# Granola Bar Devotionals

## Spiritual Snacks on the Go!

Edited and Compiled by
Alisa Hope Wagner

Scripture references marked as AMP, ESV, KJV, NIV, NKJV, NLT and the Message translations as they appear on Biblegateway.com.

Cover designed by Alisa Hope Wagner
Published by Marked Writers Publishing
www.alisahopewagner.com

ISBN: 9781728690735

# Granola Bar Devotionals

## Spiritual Snacks on the Go!

# Dedication

My spirit overflows with delight as I usher this book into publication. This project has been a grand undertaking, which is why it has taken over 12 years to birth. But the time spent guiding this ministry has shaped me and my writing more than any one project. So I am honored to give of my time, talent and energy freely to see this book realized.

This book is a project with a two-passion heart. First, every writer has donated her work, time and energy, giving the proceeds of this book to African Missions. Real mouths being fed. Real bodies being clothed. Real hearts being tended. And real souls being saved.

Second, this book is published in honor of Jeannie De La Garza—a woman whose written words will live beyond her untimely death. Jeannie embodies why we write devotionals—to leave a lasting legacy of faith to the world behind us. She has done just that, and I feel her cheering us on from heaven.

I am truly in awe that God would use this book as a support pillar for African Missions. We may not be called to be the actual hands and feet serving in distant lands, but God can use our talents in unique ways to fund, pray and encourage missionaries. When you purchase this book, you support missionaries with the money they need to complete the work for which they have been called. So thank you. Please check out the missionary website and pray for their efforts: www.gosendjoin.us

I want to thank Patricia Coughlin, Kerry Johnson and Holly Smith for your edits. You bless me with your time and talent. Also, to my sister, Shay Lee, thank you for gathering and formatting our Writers portion of the book. Your help was severely needed and greatly appreciated.

Finally, I am so grateful to all of my dear writers—whom I also call my friends. You have trusted me with your precious words, and I pray that I have done you proud. May they bless every reader with a boost of faith and a dash of joy.

Finally, not all the devotionals from *enLIVEn Devotionals Ministry* could fit in this book. There are many more encouraging faith stories to be read. You can find them and more at *enLIVEn Devotionals:* www.enlivendevotionals.com. Please be on the look-out for our current and future publications.

Alisa Hope Wagner
*Marked Writers Publishing*
www.alisahopewagner.com

# Forward

"Walk with God now, and then for eternity...." these are the words my mom inscribed in a Bible for me as a child. I don't know where she heard it spoken that way or if she came up with it on her own. The beautiful simplicity and seamless walk of the Believer moving from this life into the next sums up her life beautifully. Since her childhood, and until her passing, her greatest love was always Jesus Christ. I can confidently say she was crazy in love with our dad, head-over-heals for her children, and adored her grandchildren beyond belief. In fact, my mom was my best friend, and I still feel "lost" without her.

However, her love for Jesus was as much a part of every cell in her body as was her own DNA—there was no Jeannie without her beloved Jesus. My mom absolutely craved His presence, and she truly never lost her child-like faith. I think of Jesus' words admonishing His disciples to allow the children to come to Him. I believe that Jesus was also talking about people, like Mom, who are humble to their core in His presence. Mom's heart went out to anyone hurting and in need, but she never wanted any attention on herself.

I believe in life it is extremely rare to feel that another person is "listening" and cares, really cares, about another's pain. Mom was one of those rare gems. I look now at her journals, and they are filled with the prayer requests that she was constantly working on, even up to the weekend of her untimely passing.

Despite being a prayer warrior, she was cloaked with humility, and wanted only God glorified for His mighty works.

I know people could see these wonderful traits—realizing what an authentic, rare woman of God she was. What people did not know is that she, like so many silent sufferers, battled depression. She was faced with many adversities, and by no means had always had an easy life. However, her adoration for Jesus was grounded in Who He was, not in life's circumstances.

In 2006, when Alisa invited Mom to the very first meeting of the *Granola Bar Devotional,* Mom was so very excited for this opportunity to discuss God's Word. She would end up always taking 2-3 Bibles with her to each meeting! Nonetheless, she was also a very private soul. Since the purpose of the devotionals is for contributors to share a piece of themselves in written form (at whatever level a person is comfortable), she felt this was an obstacle for her. Though it may not have been evident to anyone present, writing in this way placed her immensely outside of her "comfort zone."

She was so excited for the ministry, but did not think she would be able to write anything for people to read. This extreme discomfort was due to the fact that she didn't want to ever write a devotional that would seem pretentious or in any way misinterpret God's Word. Through a beautiful transformation, though, I saw Mom's confidence in what she was writing absolutely flourish. She made wonderful friendships and was always excited to share with me the latest devotionals and growth of this ministry. She developed many special bonds that will endure forever—Alisa being at the top of this list.

Despite Mom's natural tendency to be way too hard on herself, she wrote devotionals that were tender and cherished, and she developed her unique voice. She realized that if any of her writings helped even one person, she was absolutely willing to step outside of her comfort zone. Mom's beautiful devotionals are one of the most precious pieces of her legacy for her family and friends. I know that these continue to reach people whom she has never met, and only Jesus truly knows all those who have been touched by Mom's writings, including the anonymous writings that even I don't know are hers. I do know that one day in Heaven Mom will meet these people.

My mom was absolutely a once-in-a-lifetime woman, and there is not a day that goes by in which I don't yearn for her presence and feel such honor in being her daughter. But I realize that we all have something that is once-in-a-lifetime within us, and God wants us to share that with everyone! This is the simple and profound beauty of the *Granola Bar Devotional.* God will use any of us, no matter how big or small we feel we are. We all have beautiful stories to tell. Thank you, Mama, for being obedient to God's calling, even when it would have been easier to stay in your comfort zone! We will meet again soon, and I love you forever.

Tammi Slavin
Laura Campise

Jeannie De La Garza
8/6/1953-6/1/2008

# God's Preparation

Tammy Andrus

Over 20 years ago when Wayne and I first surrendered our lives to loving Jesus, we were a mess. Wayne, who had been adopted at 13 years old because of neglect and abuse, was carrying baggage, and I was carrying around my baggage from living in a dysfunctional home, as well.

We were a double-fold, dysfunctional couple. If our peers were to choose a couple that was least likely for God to use, we would've been at the top of that list.

I am so thankful that God takes the broken things and makes them new. All of those terrible things that happened to us as children was God's preparation for the special work He had in store for us. It is because of our past that God is able to use us in our African mission work today.

Whatever struggles you are going through right now trust that God will use them to prepare you for your future. Allow Him to take your suffering and use it for His good.

"God saved you by his grace when you believed. And you can't take credit for this; it is a gift from God. Salvation is not a reward for the good things we have done, so none of us can boast about it. For we are God's masterpiece. He has created us anew in Christ Jesus, so we can do the good things he planned for us long ago" (Ephesians 2:8-10 NLT).

*Father, I know that I am imperfect, but I trust that you are shaping me into Your masterpiece. I understand that the struggles I face daily or preparation for my God-given destiny. Thank You for loving me so much that You would take time to love, correct and teach me.*

# The Thank You Note

Alisa Hope Wagner

A thank you note rests on my desk—the cheery picture of flowers springs up from the cover. The words inside from a friend blessed by a small gift I sent her are written with her own hand. I have received and given many thank you notes, but one in particular changed my life.

I started a small writing group about twelve years ago. We wrote devotionals—hearts crying out to the Lord. One woman struggled with being personal. Laying her soul bare on paper caused her hesitation, yet she overcame her fear in order to share God's love with others. Her two daughters also wrote for my group—young women supporting their mother's desire to share her faith through written words.

One day, I walked through a Christian book store, and I spied a lovely journal. "Send it to her," I felt the Holy Spirit say. The image of my writing friend came to mind.

I bought the journal and a card. I don't know what I wrote to her, but I'm sure it was something about writing with courage. I mailed it to her. She mailed a thank you note back. Nothing special. Simple deeds of friendship.

A few months later my friend died. It was sudden. She was too young. I spoke at her funeral—one of the hardest speeches I had ever given in my life. My words seemed so trivial—unable to capture my friend's beautifully lived life. But her daughters were grateful.

Before I left, the eldest daughter grabbed my hand. She told me that her mother, who normally was very private, poured out her soul onto the pages of a journal. She had written my name on the inside cover, honored that I had thought of her. In just a few short months, she had shared the beauty and brokenness of her life.

That journal was one of the daughter's most prized possession—a piece of her mother's heart written down in words. A small gesture. A simple gift. A fleeing moment. A prompting obeyed can make a huge impact.

Like I said. It changed my life. Now when I feel the Holy Spirit prompt me to do this or to say that, I try to obey.

"You are my friends if you do what I command" (John 15:14 NLT).

*God, let me not overlook the seemingly small things that can make a huge impact. Help me not to be so busy or so self-preoccupied that I miss the little opportunities to bless others.*

# Kudzu Vine

### Kerry Johnson

We were in our backyard on a muggy summer evening. Our two boys bounced on the trampoline, and I had just tugged another handful of unwelcome weeds from the yard when I heard my older son Cole's question.

"Is that a vine?"

I knew the exact plant he was asking about. It reached like long green arms through the top of the medium-sized oak trees behind our home. I had recently noticed that particular vine invader all over the place—not just in our backyard—its relentless green fingers growing through the tops of the trees, peeking above even the tallest of the tall.

If you drive the interstates in Florida, you're likely to notice it as well. It can top lofty Florida pines and blanket sprawling oaks, this ruthless winding vine that is pleasing to the eye but ultimately deadly to the tree it covers.

It's called the kudzu vine, and it's a common sight in parts of Georgia and Florida. Kudzu is native to Japan, and was introduced in the United States at the Philadelphia Centennial Exposition in 1876 for a variety of helpful farming reasons.

Today, however, kudzu is recognized as an invasive species that will grow over anything in its path, whether it's a tree, building, or vehicle. If you look up kudzu on the Internet, pictures show the power of this pretty yet persistent green vine as it smothers everything around it, eventually killing what it has climbed because it blocks out life-giving sunlight.

*How like worry, Lord.*

How like the cares of this present world kudzu is. Seemingly harmless, until those cares grow, and grow, and grow. Until they take over, blocking out His life-giving light and smothering the peace our faith in God assures us.

Sometimes those cares are valid, in-your-face, painfully real…a terminal family member, a lost job, a forever-strained marriage…heavy vines that seem to grow nonstop. Worries that wrap and wrangle our hearts.

But their winding, wrapping pain can't negate God's power or smother His grace. Jesus promises all Believers that we don't have to worry because He is always with us.

"Come to Me, all *you* who labor and are heavy laden, and I will give you rest. Take My yoke upon you and learn from Me, for I am gentle and lowly in heart, and you will find rest for your souls. For My yoke *is* easy and My burden is light" (Matthew 11:28-30 NKJV).

*God, You have given Your Son and the Helper—the Holy Spirit—upon Whom we can daily hand over our invasive vines of worry, to be cut off and uprooted in order to regain His light and His peace. Thank You for taking all of our burdens and worries and making them light.*

# Love is Not a Doormat

Holly Smith

Doormats are handy things—dusting off the snow before entering a somewhat-clean floor, wiping off the mud from the now-melted snow. Doormats are weathered. They can be pretty and decorative until the above happens and they become grubby. Doormats are lasting. We usually keep the same doormat by each door until we move. Then we finally throw them out, like old rags.

Whether it's learned behavior, taught behavior or even caught behavior, we act like Christians must in every way be doormats to be Christ-like. Compliance is the anchor we drag around everywhere we go. Sometimes, I feel like a doormat, don't you?

One day I shifted the lens of my perspective, though blurred with the mud wiped across my face. I began to see that even though it is not all about me—well, it isn't all about them either. To be humble, I can still be emptied of pride and callousness in my thinking and actions. I can be both humble and not walked upon.

My boundaries were like the snow-blown fences that no longer worked. I realized that I did not have to walk *with* someone to love them or to pray for them. I could stop moving toward them when I encountered them, standing still and being loving and humble and kind; yet, not moving one single inch.

Jesus showed it best in His actions. He spoke the truth in love. He had boundaries with people. For some, He let them in close to see more of Him. He told those closest that He would submit Himself to being crucified. He was willing. He had strength that could overcome all obstacles, and He chose to be crucified. Changed before the disciples' eyes, Jesus was taken to Heaven to live forever—to continue to intercede on our behalf.

He humbled Himself on that cross. The whole time, He was strength under control. He looked outward, prayed for and loved others. He was killed. But it didn't last! Three days later, Jesus arose, conquering sin and death! Within the infinite scope of His ability, He took upon Himself the sins of the world and He submitted His material being to death—resurrecting immaterial, immortal, Immanuel—the spotless Lamb of God. Not once, not one single time, was Jesus a doormat. He was a Victor!

"For this is how God loved the world: He gave his one and only Son, so that everyone who believes in him will not perish but have eternal life" (John 3:16 NLT).

*Father, help me to see the value You have in me. I don't have to be a doormat to be called Your child. Thank You for loving me so much that You would send Jesus to die for my sins, so I could have a relationship with You.*

# God's Perfect Path

Liette Ocker

My husband and I were in total shock as we learned our two-year-old son was severely hearing impaired, and that a battery of medical tests were still needed. Immediately following the appointment, I dropped my son off at his daycare and went to fulfill a volunteer commitment I had previously agreed to. I was so confused.

I wondered why I had chosen to leave my son after learning he is nearly deaf. Wouldn't a normal mother in this situation want to hold and comfort her child instead of leave him behind, especially since I knew I could easily get out of my commitment with a simple phone call? I did not know why I was doing it, but I just wanted to run away from my child and his problem that I knew I could never fix.

I just wanted so desperately to keep my mind busy, so I would not have to think about the seemingly impossible life-sentence my son was just given. In the midst of my confusion, I did not see that God had a perfect plan, and He knew exactly what I would need that day. I drove right into the arms of one of the godliest couples I have ever met.

I told this dear couple about our son's hearing tests, and they prayed for my family and our son. Immediately the burden on my heart lifted. God knew that these two wonderful people would provide the love and support necessary to minimize my problems and maximize our God.

Although that morning I did not think it was possible, I spent the rest of the day thoroughly enjoying the fellowship provided by God through two amazing people.

"As for God, His way is perfect! The word of the Lord is tested and tried; He is a shield to all those who take refuge and put their trust in Him" (Psalm 18.30 NIV).

*Thank You, God, for providing me with the perfect path, even when I do not know where it is leading. Help me to take refuge in You and to trust You in every area of my life.*

# A Family's Salvation

Tammy Andrus

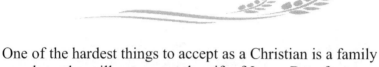

One of the hardest things to accept as a Christian is a family member who will not accept the gift of Jesus. But after years of praying for my family and sharing God's love, I began to see God's hand at work. My little brother began to have random people tell him that he needed to give his life to Christ.

One night while escaping from a friend's house that was being robbed at gunpoint, my brother ran to a house for help. In the middle of the house's yard was a large sign that read, "Jesus Saves." The owner of the house helped my brother, and the following day, the man called to check on him.

The man began to tell my brother about Jesus' love and sacrifice for us. The man also told my brother that he needed to give his life to the Lord. About six months later while talking to my best friend about my brother, I found out that he was the same man that she had been witnessing to for some time now.

My friend and her family would specifically visit with my brother and witness to him. I realized that I wasn't the only person praying for my brother's salvation. His salvation was also in my friend and her family's prayers. Though the process was long, my brother finally became a Christian. Through the prayers and actions of compassionate Christians, he finally received Christ as his Lord and Savior.

Now my brother and I have teamed up and are praying for the salvation of the rest of our family, and though the process may take a while, we know that God's love will eventually touch their hearts.

"Brothers, children of Abraham, and you God-fearing Gentiles, it is up to us that this message of salvation has been sent" (Acts 13:26 NIV).

*Father, You know that it is upsetting for us when we have family members that have not accepted You as their Lord and Savior. Please help us to diligently pray for our lost loved ones and show us how we can share Your love in a gentle way.*

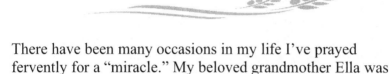

# Spiritual Amnesia

### Sofia J. Lyons

There have been many occasions in my life I've prayed fervently for a "miracle." My beloved grandmother Ella was rushed to the ER as the EMT tried to revive her 63-year-old lifeless body.

We got the call from New York from a frantic aunt saying they don't know if she's going to make it! I ran to my bedroom collapsing on the floor and prayed fervently, "Dear Lord please spare my beautiful grandmother, Ella, who is like a mother to so many."

I was in such emotional despair as a teenager and new Christian, and my deep prayers and steady flow of teardrops felt like I was sweating drops of blood. My Miracle didn't come and Ella died at 63 years old. My hero was gone.

Although that prayer wasn't answered the way I'd hoped, it did not deter me from continuing to ask God for miracles. Many times since that day over twenty-five years ago, God has answered my prayers. There was the IRS miracle, where my bill was reduced 75% after praying fervently while my husband "bartered" with the IRS on the telephone for over three hours! We were told that the IRS never barters with anyone, but I prayed, asking for the miracle and we received it—saving us over $10,000 and great stress financially!

There was Howie the Jewish atheist who was in the adult entertainment industry and had a heart made of stone. His family was far away, and they asked if I would visit his bedside since I was the only person they knew in New York. Howie and I talked, and the Holy Spirit's presence was strong in his hospital room. As we talked and prayed, his heart melted and he prayed to accept Christ in his hospital bed one day before his death in that same hospital room.

How then can I ever worry about the next big problem to come along and doubt God can handle it when I have solid proof of His hand working out miracles before my own eyes? I cannot forget the big and small ways God has showed up for me as if I was suffering from spiritual amnesia!

"So do not worry, saying, 'What shall we eat?' or 'What shall we drink?' or 'What shall we wear?' For the pagans run after all these things, and your heavenly Father knows that you need them. But seek first his kingdom and his righteousness, and all these things will be given to you as well" (Matthew 6:31-33 NIV).

*Heavenly Father, help me to always remember how You have been with me every step of the way during my life journey on this earth. Let me never forget that the Holy Spirit is always with me, especially during the times that are difficult and painful.*

# His Peace

Sunny Reed

God's peace is different from our idea of peace. I am due to have our third baby any day now, and our home has been full of family and friends helping us out. At the same time, my two little girls have become a little uneasy knowing change is on the way.

After a disastrous breakfast replete with spankings, crying, a distressed Grandma and an exhausted Mommy, I sought solace under my covers with my Bible and begged God for some peace as I drank in His Scriptures. His words were like a cool river running through my body, calming me down, bringing me peace and strengthening me for the rest of the day. That morning I could feel the power of His Word, and I knew that it was the only Bread from which we can live on.

However, the following morning resembled much of the previous, and I found myself begging Jesus to please give this house some peace. This went on for most of the week. The girls' unstable emotions erupted frequently. I was embarrassed when my daughters acted as though they had not been taught a single manner in their whole life. It wasn't until I sat in church today that the light bulb finally came on.

I was worshiping God, totally focused on Him and completely able to relax regardless of distractions around me or in my head. I was so content sitting in that chair eating up the worship, hearing God's voice and receiving good teaching. I realized how relaxed I was and wondered for a minute how I had come to this foreign state of mind. I realized then and there that when I had asked God for peace, He had given it to me.

His peace didn't necessarily mean my girls behaved magically or my house cleaned itself. This peace came from within and it had sustained me all week. I love how God answers us in His way and am thankful I have His Bread for strength snacking.

"Mercy, peace and love be yours in abundance" (Jude 1:2 NIV).

*Father, please help me to have Your peace even though the world around me is chaotic. I pray that peace will overflow me, spilling into my home and into the hearts of my family. Thank You for blessing us with the gift of peace and making it available to us whenever we ask. Please show me how to find peace in the storm.*

# The Gift

Susan Wood

Every time the Lord speaks to me any bit of wisdom or sends me a message through someone else, I think of it as a gift to me. If someone gave me rubies and gold, it wouldn't mean as much as one piece of wisdom from my Lord.

*I received a gift today.* I feel like I say that so much to myself. Each gift seems better than the last—each so bright and shiny, each has its own niche and characteristic. Today's gift was so special because God used my exact wording to speak a message to me.

While watching Joyce Meyer this morning, Joyce used the same words I have been using in my private prayers to the Lord, along with a wonderful teaching about it. The crazy thing is, whenever God answers my private prayers with such accuracy, I get more excited that He would make the motion to answer me than the actual answer.

His motive behind His motion to me is even more spectacular than the answer to my question or situation. Through His motion to answer, I can see His heart. His private words to me are like precious jewels. I feel like I have a great big treasure chest that I store all of His priceless jewels that He gives to me.

Years ago, young women would have hope chests filled with special items in anticipation of their future marriage. In the Bible Jesus makes many references to us as His bride and to a glorious celebration and wedding feast we will one day participate in.

My treasure chest is my personal hope chest, where, along with His words, I store all my hopes and dreams of my eternity with Him.

"The kingdom of heaven is like treasure hidden in a field. When a man found it, he hid it again, and then in his joy went and sold all he had and bought that field" (Matthew 13:44 NIV).

*Father, thank You for the amazing treasures that You give me each and every day. Help me to slow down and keep my ears attentive to Your 'motions' in my life. I know that you have a chest full of awesome insights for me.*

# Shaping the Future

Laura Campise

I was recently out with a group of my friends celebrating the upcoming wedding of our close friend. I was having a wonderful dinner and enjoying the time of relaxation and fellowship. As the night wore on, the conversation turned to our children and the joy and craziness of motherhood. We began to talk about how challenging it can be with the daily grind of taking care of the little ones, doing the laundry, cleaning the house, etc.

We also discussed how easy it was for us to wonder what we were contributing to this world. I think this is very common for many women and something that I really struggled with after having my son. Before I became a mom, I was used to my identity being wrapped up nicely in my job, in the areas that I volunteered and in physical exercise.

I think that regardless of whether a woman is a stay-at-home-mom or she works outside the home, she may question whether or not she is contributing to society. God has really been working on this issue with me as I have struggled to find my purpose and to feel that my life is important. I have heard it said so many times that as mothers we are amazingly powerful and influential. I am sure we have all heard the saying, "The hand that rocks the cradle rules the world."

We are literally shaping this next generation. This is something that has taken a hold in my heart. What an amazing responsibility. I know I make a difference every time I play with my son, read him a book or pray over him at night. I am shaping his future. Being a mother is not about giving up and sacrificing our dreams; it is about helping the next generation accomplish their dreams by giving them everything they need emotionally and spiritually, so that one day make their own mark on this world.

"Love the LORD your God with all your heart and with all your soul and with all your strength. These commandments that I give you today are to be upon your hearts. Impress them on your children. Talk about them when you sit at home and when you walk along the road, when you lie down and when you get up" (Deuteronomy 6:5-7 NIV).

*Lord, thank You so much for entrusting me with Your child/children. I pray that I honor You as I live my life out before them. Help me to be an example of You to them. Help me to make my mark in this life.*

# A Royal Princess

## A.J. Pattengill

A true princess knows who she is in Christ Jesus. I am not referring to Disney-character princesses with their false sense of attention or the beautiful American Meagan Markle princess that we all watched live on television as she married her Prince Harry. They are the world's standard of royalty, but a true princess is something far better.

The Bible's standard of a true princess is that she gets wisdom from the Word, she defends the truth, she humbly serves, she loves good and hates evil and she loves the Lord. It is for these qualities that she has earned the praise of many nations. True royalty is not characterized by robes worn or thrones occupied, but by a faithful obedience to the most Royal King of Kings. We have been called to be royal priesthood, a holy nation, and we embrace that royalty by honoring our Lord the King who gave us His royal lineage.

On my recent mission trip, I came upon a sweet little girl who had never seen or heard a violin. I was playing in a Guatemala village of Central America. This little girl walked up to me very curious about my instrument. I kneeled down to my knees to get to her level to make eye contact with this innocent creature. While I played for her, Jesus spoke to my heart and said: "This little girl is My princess." Someone in my group took a photo of that moment, and you can certainly see in the photo that she is the King's princess. In fact, every girl is God's daughter and His royal princess. It does not matter her culture or background or if she's wealthy or poor. If she believes that Christ Jesus, the Son of God, is her true Lord and Savior, she is by biblical standards a princess.

"But you are a chosen people, a royal priesthood, a holy nation, God's special possession, that you may declare the praises of him who called you out of darkness into his wonderful light" (1 Peter 2:9 NIV).

*Father, help me to fully understand and embrace what Your Word says about me. I am a royal princess because I am Your daughter, and I've accepted Jesus Christ as my Lord and Savior. I want to pass on this truth to other young women and girls who needs to see themselves as they truly are: A princess.*

# Italian Food Lesson

Teresa Ann

It was a day we were craving Italian. Let's just say the craving got its way as we showed up to our favorite Italian restaurant. Anticipation and expectation of a great time was short-lived as we walked through the doors. It felt as though we had walked into an invisible wall of a "joy vacuum."

Have you ever experienced something like that before? You know the moment where you enter an atmosphere that permeates oppression? We were "greeted" with a monotone voice accompanied with eyes half closed and arms crossed and an "Eyore'ish" attitude.

I began to quickly feel the hot temperature rise within me as I formulated what I was going to say, but the Holy Spirit whispered, "Mission field moment." Suddenly, it was as though everything stopped. Time seemed to stand still as I was getting a lesson that I would remember for the rest of my life. It was as though I heard, "You've prayed for your city, Teresa…well, this is one in your city that I'm highlighting. Now let Me love her through you."

Think about that moment or perhaps moments you've been in that were incredibly similar. Those moments you felt that your joy was being stolen. Yet, that day was a day where my world again got flipped "right side up," as God showed me His perspective. He was reminding me, "Yes there are attacks everywhere on the Kingdom of God. However, Teresa, the Kingdom of God does not take offense. The Kingdom of God is righteousness, joy and peace in Me and My Holy Spirit."

I continued to hear these words in my heart: "Respond to Me versus reacting to them. For love is the greatest gift, and I am Love!" And I began to see the words from a multitude of Scriptures encouraging me to step in love. Yet, in those short moments, my mind tried to reason myself out of His love by thinking.

"I don't want to be a doormat by just being love." However, right after that fleeting thought I felt God say, "I Am not a pushover! My love is the most powerful gift. It's a weapon that rescues. When you operate in Me and My Love, you're not a doormat. Instead, you become a "welcome mat" to invite Me, the King of Kings into people's lives."

"He has shown you, O mortal, what is good. And what does the LORD require of you? To act justly and to love mercy and to humbly with your God" (Micah 6.8 NIV).

*Father, in those moments of difficulty with others, I am quickly reminded of this lesson of love from the greatest Teacher of Teachers. Help me to be an invitation for others to meet the King of all Kings. I know that I will never be the same and neither will they of I respond in Your love.*

# One True Thing

### Kimberly Dawn Rempel

Hands clutching a mug of sweet coffee, I pinch my eyes closed to hear sounds like the ocean streaming through the tree leaves. Wind sways them like waves. I open my eyes to return to the reality of my neighborhood. Far above it all, wind pushes thick layers of grey cloud toward the single patch of blue sky. I consider how it must look above the clouds—sunny and clear, a perfect day.

The patch of blue shrinks and is swallowed by a sky of grey. All is cloudy and gloomy from where I sit, yet I know the sky above has not changed. It is still blue, sunny and clear—just hidden from my view. I understand Solomon's rants about how life is in many ways useless or unfair or impossible to understand.

"Meaningless! Meaningless!" says the Teacher. "Utterly meaningless! Everything is meaningless" (Ecclesiasts 1:2 NIV).

My feelings, views and beliefs seem real and concrete to me but are, in fact, full of deception. They change based on circumstance or as I gain new understanding. How, then, can I maintain any opinion, belief or feeling when it may not be real or true? What can I rely on?

The only constant is our unchanging God. "He is the same yesterday, today and forever." What I feel, believe or understand won't ever change who He is or His plans for me. As I know God more and more, I become more confident of who I am and my purpose, and I am assured that He is the one right thing. He is true. He is good. He is alive and real.

Sometimes I can't see Him beyond my grey clouds of misunderstanding, but He's still there and still the same. Of all the things I'll never know or understand this is one thing I can know for sure. God is real and good and unchanging.

"Jesus Christ is the same yesterday, today and forever" (Hebrews 13:8 NLT).

*Thank You, Lord, that You are the same yesterday, today and forever. My sight is clouded by the worries of this life and sin, misunderstanding, guilt, lies, selfishness, pride. Please forgive me for believing these lies instead of Your Truth. Lord, thank You for opening my eyes more and more as you reveal Yourself to me.*

## God's Representative

Susie Mozisek

I believe that every day we have choices to show Christ's love. Today that opportunity came as I was picking up a few items at our neighborhood grocery store. I approached the checkout stand knowing full well that I had basically five minutes to pick up my daughter from school. Looking at the three person line in front of me, I had to make a choice. Should I go for the express lane even though I had too many items, should I ask someone if I could go in front of them, or should I just be late picking up my daughter?

Suddenly, my knight-in-shining-armor came forward and said, "I'm opening another line. Who's next?"

Trying not to hurt anyone, I quickly made my way over but was a millisecond behind my competition. I begged, "Could I please go first. I am supposed to pick up my daughter from school in five minutes."

Prepared to give her a huge thanks, my smile quickly turned upside down as she rolled her eyes at me and started to say something rude. I stopped her before she could finish. I said, "Never mind. That's okay."

I walked back to my line of three and sulked. The cashier was pretty quick and it was finally my turn to check out. I was putting my groceries on the conveyer when I looked behind me and saw the sweetest old man smiling patiently with a single link of sausage. He was obviously in no hurry, but I had a decision to make. Was I going to be like the extremely selfish lady before (not that I'm bitter or anything) or was I going to be nice and let him go ahead of me?

*Okay God, I know that this is an opportunity to show love to others.* Of course, I let him go in front. The checker got me out in one minute flat. I ran to my car, threw the groceries in and actually made it to the school while there was still a line of cars picking up. I looked down as I was sitting in my car and noticed I was wearing my church's t-shirt.

Unknowingly, I was representing everyone at my church with my actions today. I just smiled and knew that God was smiling too.

"In all your ways acknowledge him, and he will make your paths straight" (Proverbs 3:6 NIV).

*Heavenly Father, help me to acknowledge You in every area of my life. I want to exemplify Your goodness in all my actions.*

# Wood Block

Estella Smith

One night I was lying in bed and whining to God. *Why God? Why do bad things happen? Why can't they be avoided—both the things that we choose and things we didn't choose.* I sat there thinking about all the things I have experienced in my life.

I told God that I feel that all these negative experiences have chipped away at who I am and who I'm supposed to be. I feel weak when I should feel strong or hesitant when I should move. Why do things have to be difficult at times? Then God so gently answered as He always does. (Not the kind of reaction my kids get from me when they whine. God is so loving!)

He revealed to me a picture in my mind: it was of a block of wood. Then He said to me that sometimes it does hurt when experiences and trials feel as if they are chipping away at us, but every chip is shaping us. Every chip brings the piece of wood closer to being the piece of art that God has intended for us.

The finished product is beautiful artwork; and without certain experiences to chip away at the block of wood, we won't become the finished product we are called to be. Instead of whining about the hard times, I should rejoice because they are making me beautiful in His eyes.

"But he knows the way that I take; when he has tested me, I will come forth as gold" (Job 23:10 NIV).

*Lord, please keep me strong. Keep me focused through difficult times. Help me to have peace when I do not understand. I desire to be the beautiful piece of artwork that You want me to be. There is purpose in all things, and Your Glory will shine through. Please show me how to be strong as You chisel my life.*

# Can You Hear God?

Tiffany Molina

My 5-year-old son asked me after we came home from church last week, "Mommy, how do we know God is talking to us if we can't hear him?"

This seemed to him and to me a fair question to ask. I had to think about how I would answer him. I laughed first at how cute he was and then said, "Well, you just have to be really quiet and listen to your heart where God speaks to us the most."

He and I have been very committed to our new relationship with God and our church. I am proud of his question because I know he is wondering about his faith. I asked him if he understood what I meant, and he said, "Yes, Mommy."

He then went on to tell me how he loves church. "It's fun right, Mom?" he asked.

"Yes, Buddy, church is great!" I said.

It's nice when our children in all their innocence remind us of what others can't see, or hear in this case. We can hear God. He is there to heal us when we are hurt and guide us when we are lost. We just have to listen. I am sure children aren't the only ones who wonder if God is really there. I'm glad to know He is.

"But Jesus called the children to him and said, "Let the little children come to me, and do not hinder them, for the kingdom of God belongs to such as these" (Luke 18:16 NIV).

*Dear God, please help me to always hear Your Words and always be ready to listen. Thank You for the innocent questions of my children. They remind me that You are always with us.*

# Clark's Prayer

Cynthia Faulkner

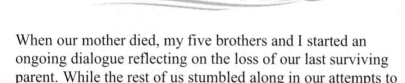

When our mother died, my five brothers and I started an ongoing dialogue reflecting on the loss of our last surviving parent. While the rest of us stumbled along in our attempts to comfort each other amidst our own grief, my brother Clark would simply say, "Let's pray."

I recall one prayer he led with me that went like this: "Dear God. Help Pat in Heaven. Amen."

You have to know my brother to understand the significance of this simple prayer. Clark took care of my mother as she deteriorated over time from her diabetes. He lived with her until she was placed in a nursing home after her second leg was amputated and she was determined legally blind. While in the nursing home, Clark called our mother every morning and evening to check in with her.

The rest of us siblings were not as devoted in our contacts with our mother and we allowed our busy lives to excuse this bad behavior. But Clark was ever faithful, both in keeping in touch with mom and in praying for her. This may not seem significantly different than the average American family except that my brother may not fit the common definition of average.

He was born with Downs Syndrome. Even in his simplistic world, Clark understood the comforting value of prayer.

"Be joyful in hope, patient in affliction, faithful in prayer" (Romans 12:12 NIV).

*Dear Heavenly Father, I turn over all my pain and distress to Your capable care and I find comfort that You are in control. Help me not to worry and grieve about the difficulties in life. Show me how to be faithful in prayer.*

# Thank God for Aunt Seennie

Jeannie De La Garza

My mother, Jo Ann, grew up in post-Depression rural Kansas. She was a very sad and frightened little girl. Her family was falling apart, and she felt that she was completely alone. However, we now see the hand of God in her life even at an early age. At the age of five, Jo Ann would walk to school every day.

Along that route was located her Great Aunt Seennie's home. Aunt Seennie knew of Jo Ann's family circumstances, and she always greeted Jo Ann before school and welcomed her inside for lunch. She spent this time introducing Jo Ann to Someone she did not know—Someone who loved her unconditionally and would never leave her.

Jesus was introduced to my mother's life during those precious visits. And because of Seennie's efforts, my family's lineage has been forever changed. Aunt Seennie simply gave my mother what she could. There were no eloquent prayers or deep theological discussions. Seennie simply taught my mother how to pray directly to her loving Father in Jesus' name.

I believe that even without Aunt Seennie, my mother would have eventually come to know Jesus, but Seennie also gave my mother love and comfort during a time that she needed it most.

To this day, my mother has one of the deepest relationships with Jesus of anyone I have ever known. She still prays the way she was taught—with wonderful, childlike faith.

My prayer is that I will continue Aunt Seennie and Mom's legacy and simply share Jesus with those who need Him.

"Be very careful, then, how you live – not as unwise but as wise, making the most of every opportunity, because the days are evil" (Ephesians 5:15-16 NIV).

*Father, thank You for others who have obeyed Your call and have influenced my family forever. Please help me to also seize the opportunities that You put before me. Today, show me where I can be a witness for You.*

# God's Plan for Parents

Ann Cornelius

One of the joys of getting older is seeing the fruits of your labor. For Christian parents it is especially good to see your grown children living out the faith passed down from generations. In 1972, my son was born after a difficult breach birth. He was premature weighing 4 pounds and 11 ounces. This child was dedicated to the Lord from the beginning.

He had difficulty breathing properly. When the doctor told me he might not live, I turned to God in prayer. Our church family prayed for his life to be spared. He slowly gained strength and after ten days in the hospital, he was released to go home. At night while my husband and I took turns feeding him, our prayers would float up from full hearts to Jesus.

My child grew and became a little boy with a heart for the Lord. We had a weekly Bible club at our house, and each week children would come to our Good News Club. The children got to listen to Bible stories with flannel graph figures and sing songs about Jesus and His love.

At times, it seemed like a lot of trouble, but then I would be encouraged by the children asking Jesus into their hearts. One day it was quite rainy, and the club had four children: my two children and two others. In a moment, I had a sense of foresight that God had a special purpose for their lives. My son, Bil, was especially sensitive to the other children no matter who came. He wanted them to come to our Good News Club and would invite all the kids at his school.

That was the beginning of his call to be a soul winner. Today, my son is pastor of *Church Unlimited* in Corpus Christi, Texas. The other boy in club that day is a fulltime drama minister and travels with a well-known gospel singer. The two girls are Christian mothers and career professionals. Who knew that one little Bible club could make such a difference in the lives of children.

"Train up a child in the way he should go, and when he is old, he will not turn from it" (Proverbs 22:6 NIV).

*Father, I thank You for using me to share Your love with my children and others through the years. Thank You for Your hand on my life in winning and influencing souls for Your kingdom. Help me to continually obey Your leading. Now open my eyes to witnessing opportunities that you are currently providing.*

# A+ Intimacy

## Alisa Hope Wagner

I recently found out that my 11-year-old son is doing poorly in literature. He has failed the last two quizzes over his assigned reading. He was frustrated that he wasn't doing well. I could tell he didn't understand why he was struggling.

So I decided to give him an analogy.

"How well do you know me?" I asked him.

"Very well," he said looking up to me.

I nodded. "Yes, I think you do, so you would have an A+ in our relationship because you know me."

He smiled.

"But how do you know me so well?" I asked.

He thought. "We spend time together. You tuck me in every night. You help me with my homework. We talk," he suggested.

"Exactly!" I exclaimed. "You have an A+ because you spend time with me."

49

Now I looked at him seriously. "Do you spend a lot of time with your literature homework?"

"No," he said, looking slightly embarrassed.

"If you don't read your book assignments and get to know the story, will you do well on the quizzes?"

He shook his head.

"You have a failing grade in literature because you don't know the information very well. If you want to do well, you will need to spend time with the book and get to know it, right?"

"Yes," he whispered.

I hugged him. "It will take time, but once you get to know the story, you will do well on the quizzes."

I just found out today that he got an A+ on his literature quiz. It's been almost two weeks and his grade is already improving. He's getting to know the information, so he's empowered to do well.

This story reminds me of a truth that many people miss. We can't expect the fullness of God's power, peace and provision in our lives if we don't get to know Him. Many times we want these A+ relationships with God, yet we don't read His Word, spend time with Him in prayer and listen and obey His voice.

Although we are saved by grace, and we have received an A+ as God's sons and daughters, our intimacy with Him is up to us.

God's Spirit is always available to be known and to know, but we must invest our time, energy and resources into our relationship with Him. Only then can we walk in an A+ serving of His power.

"I also pray that you will understand the incredible greatness of God's power for us who believe him. This is the same mighty power that raised Christ from the dead and seated him in the place of honor at God's right hand in the heavenly realms" (Ephesians 1:19-20 NLT).

*God, I want an intimate, deep relationships with You. Guide my time, so I can put my relationship with You first. I desire Your power in my life, so I can achieve the great plans that You have for me.*

# Holy Deafness

Dixie Phillips

My friend hurt my feelings. She spread "her view" to several other friends. Her comments waltzed their way into my house and infuriated me. I was sure I had been fatally wounded. Falling to my knees, I wailed, "Speak to me from Your Word."

I opened my Bible to the gospel of Mark: "But Jesus, not heeding the word spoken…" (Mark 5:36 ASV). It was soul food. I knew I needed "holy deafness," or I would become part of the problem, rather than part of the solution. I sat quietly and began to pray. Lord, give me holy deafness when hurtful words are said. Help me to continue to be about my Father's business and not be shipwrecked because of cruel comments that have pierced my soul.

Help me to pray as You prayed, "Father, forgive them for they know not what they do" (Luke 23:34). Sometimes, Lord, those You have called me to serve sting, and I find it difficult to wash their feet; but, You, Master, washed Judas' feet and called him, "friend." You knew from the beginning what was in his heart. Yet, You humbled Yourself and ministered to him just hours before he betrayed You.

I openly admit, Lord, that my heart sometimes resists and screams, "I can see through them!" But, You, Lord, plead with me, "See them through." My stubborn will hollers, "I'm not budging an inch." But, You, Lord, entreat me, "When they ask you to go one mile, go with them two."

I can go the second mile as long as You go with me, Lord. You make the bitter sweet. Lord, grant me holy deafness, so I can obey Your Word. I'm in earnest when I say I want to be like You. I place Your cup to my lips, Lord, and I drink. I realize it's the only way our world will ever come to know You.

You, Savior, must live out Your life through Your children. Lord, give us holy deafness to the careless conversations with those we come in contact with, but give us keen hearing to Your Holy Spirit.

"Then the righteous will shine like the sun in the kingdom of their Father. He who has ears, let him hear" (Matthew 13:43 NIV).

*Father, Lord, help me to not heed the harsh words that people can sometime say. Please show me how to have holy deafness. I want to keep my ears directed toward You, Father. Show me how to love those who hurt me.*

# She's Ready

## Vicki Beck

How can she be 18? I know it's a cliché, but it's true. It seems like only yesterday that she was just a baby. And now my baby girl has become an amazing, beautiful young lady with a love for life that matches her love for our Lord. High school graduation is behind her, and in just a few short weeks she and her most necessary and prized possessions will be moving to a university campus seven hours from our home. These days I find her sorting through boxes, drawers and endless piles trying to decide what goes to her new home in the dorm and what stays behind.

Porcelain dolls will be wrapped up and stored in the attic along with the box of dress-up clothes and miscellaneous keepsakes from her childhood. Her stereo and new TV/ DVD player, laptop and dorm-size refrigerator will make the move, along with photos of friends and family and other reminders of home.

Knowing she's the last of our four children to leave home, friends constantly ask me if I'm ready for "the empty nest." Usually I just smile and say I think so, but mostly I'm just thankful that she's ready. Not because she's had the love, support and encouragement of her family and friends, or even because she's worked hard and excelled in school. I know she's ready because she's packing her rock collection—and these are no ordinary rocks.

These rocks were claimed one Wednesday evening during a church service when hearts were anxious as our members prepared to move into a new, larger building. Pointing to a large pile of rocks, our pastor invited us to take a rock for every milestone we had experienced in our former church building, a reminder of all that God had done in our hearts and lives in that place.

Just as college is a milestone in her life, the rocks she chose symbolize a spiritual mountaintop, epiphany or covenant—milestones shared with her God. Yes, thankfully God has prepared her and me for this moment. And though I know it'll be tough letting her go, I find peace in knowing God will be with her every step of the way!

"Listen to me, you who pursue righteousness and who seek the Lord: Look to the rock from which you were cut and the quarry from which you were hewn" (Isaiah 51:1 NIV).

*Heavenly Father, lyrics from a timeless hymn repeat sweetly in my mind reminding me that You are the solid rock on which I stand, a firm foundation and security in a world that is ever changing.*

# Rewarded Obedience

### Liette Ocker

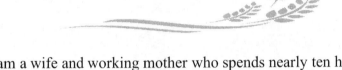

I am a wife and working mother who spends nearly ten hours a week commuting to my job. During almost every prayer, I would ask God to open up a position closer to home. One evening during First Wednesday service at my church, God told me to "stay where you are." I was devastated. How could God ask me to stay in a job that kept me from my family? I did not know the reason, but I conceded and stayed were I was.

I quit asking God to move me and started asking him to use me. A short time later, I was sitting in church praying and an image flashed into my head. I was standing in a classroom where I work, holding hands in a circle with a group of my students I had grown close with during the semester, and we were praying. I nearly fell off my chair at church. I thought that surly God did not want me to pray with my class in a government institution (I wasn't sure just how many rules that would break)!

I spent the next two days talking with God trying to convince Him that this was not a good idea. I walked to the classroom very nervous and still not sure if I would obey God's request. As I entered the room, I could not believe my eyes. One of my students was dressed exactly as I had seen her in my mind! I made my decision and announced, "Today we are going to pray."

I nervously told the class about my vision (including God showing me what the young lady would be wearing) and that I believe that God had special plans for this group. Another student—a big football player—popped up from his desk and said, "Amen, let's do it!" So we gathered around, held hands, and I said a prayer.

After class had ended, the young lady told us that she had bought that shirt she was wearing for her graduation, and that she usually tried on several outfits before deciding on the right one. However, that particular morning she grabbed her new blouse and just put it on.

If that wasn't amazing enough, one week later I received a call that a new position was just created for a job right down the street from my home! I couldn't believe what I was hearing. I knew that the job was mine because God always rewards obedience.

"In everything that [s]he undertook in the service of God's temple and in obedience to the law and the commands, [s]he sought [her] his God and worked wholeheartedly. And so [s]he prospered" (2 Chronicles 31:21 NIV).

*Dear Lord, please help me to open my heart to You and listen to Your will. Give me the courage today to obey Your requests even when I do not understand the purpose, and thank You for blessing Your faithful servants. Encourage me in the areas that I have been struggling.*

# Power of Words

## Susie Mozisek

Have you ever caught yourself repeating the words of your mother? I recently told my six-year-old daughter, "Sticks and stones may break your bones, but words will never hurt you." This is a quote my mother often sang to her very sensitive daughter, who happens to be me. I know she meant well in sharing this, but I can't understand why I would repeat such absurdity to my own daughter knowing it isn't true.

Words do hurt. They can literally change a person's attitude for better or worse. There are several negative things I can remember hearing throughout my life which have had a profound effect on how I feel about myself and my abilities. Those words were often spoken to me in haste or without thought. Many times the words were not even necessarily true. On a positive note, there are many more affirmative words I've heard, as well.

Words that told me who I am in Christ, and words that brought forth beauty and confidence. I have also been given words that tell me of a God who loves me with an everlasting love. These words weren't always spoken to me by man or woman. They were often given to me through the Holy Spirit by reading my Bible.

God has also spoken words of encouragement through my husband, my family and my friends. A kind word spoken at the right time has actually caused my heart to leap, or at least feel like it's leaping. Sometimes it will be a note of encouragement, a sweet phone call or even a beautifully written email. I don't know about you, but I want to be someone who gives joy and praise through my words.

If you have an ability to encourage someone with a kind spoken gesture, please do so. You have no idea how much it may mean, or what lasting effect it may have on them.

"Do not withhold good from those who deserve it, when it is in your power to act" (Proverbs 3:27 NIV).

*Lord, I want to thank You and praise You for Your written words in the Bible. These words guide us to understanding who You are and who You created each of us to be. Help me today to embrace the life-giving power of words. Allow me to pass on my Christian faith through my words as I speak to my family, my friends and my other relationships.*

# Master Problem Solver

### Tammi Slavin

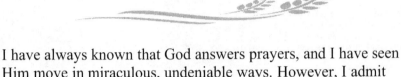

I have always known that God answers prayers, and I have seen Him move in miraculous, undeniable ways. However, I admit that I am guilty of not always bringing Him into my day-to-day challenges. I suppose I feel that I bother Him enough, and He's probably pretty busy with more important things anyway! This was my mind-set while listening to my pastor's message about allowing God to illuminate solutions.

I was having a really difficult time juggling my many responsibilities in life—mothering three children, working part-time, helping my husband with his business, doing church activities, etc. Like many women, I was feeling very overwhelmed and a little self-defeated. The main area of my life where things were coming to a head was keeping up with the housework.

I distinctly remember mopping the kitchen floor on Sunday after listening to my pastor's message and meditating on the Scripture, as well as thinking about all the things around the house that needed to be done. We women must multi-task, even if only mentally, right? I was praying very earnestly that God would show me a way to fix everything.

All of a sudden, the thought came into my mind: "Why don't I promote Briannah's household responsibilities? She's been doing the same ones for three years. And while I'm at it, I can give Richard some of Briannah's old chores. And why isn't the three-year-old helping at all?" Now this might sound like common sense to many people, but I had never thought of it!

Sometimes we're so involved with a situation that we can't see clearly the solution. This was, I know, the prompting of God giving me an answer to a problem that I could not fix myself. God truly is interested in the day-to-day operation of my life! I had been boxing Him in, assuming that He was a far-off God, not powerful enough to manage my problems.

"Do not be anxious about anything, but in everything, by prayer and petition, with thanksgiving, present your requests to God" (Philippians 4:6 NIV).

*Father, help me to remember that I should always come to You first with issues in my life. Forgive me for assuming that You don't care enough to help me in my day-to-day life.*

# Missions at 16

### Willow Andrus

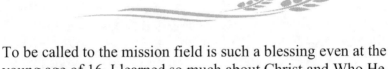

To be called to the mission field is such a blessing even at the young age of 16. I learned so much about Christ and Who He is because of the amazing opportunities He had put before me. But this isn't about me; it's about what God has done through me, and that is a story that still amazes me daily.

When I was 16 years old, my family was called to the mission field, and by my family I don't mean me. At the age of 16, I thought I knew it all, and I rebelled quite furiously against my parents' decision to move my family to Mombasa, Kenya. After hardening my heart for so long, I realized that God had me there for a reason, and I decided to make the best of my time.

I started making friends with amazing Kenyan people and other missionaries. I met moms who lost their kids. I met kids who lost their parents. Ultimately, I met so many people who still had hope despite their circumstances. God put many special people in my life who have taught me so much about Who Jesus is and how much He loves us.

I ended up gaining so much more than I could have ever imagined! After spending six months in Mombasa, my family came back to home to the states, and I became burdened for the people in Mombasa more and more every day. I tried to avoid

God's call for a while, but I finally came to terms with the fact that God has called me to the mission field.

He hasn't revealed much to me about where I will go, how long I will stay, what I will do, or how I will get the money; but I know that if God calls me, He qualifies me in every area. God has called me to "embrace the nations with Him" despite the sacrifice, despite my fear, despite what I want, and—at the end of the day—despite me.

Will you embrace the nations with God? He has not only challenged all of us, He has commanded us! Maybe that means you stay where you are and witness to your family and friends. Maybe that means writing or being an amazing mom. Maybe God is calling you to go to an unreached area or maybe God is calling you to give from your resources.

I can't tell you how He has called you, but I can guarantee that God has called you to something awesome in this life.

"He said to them, 'Go into all the world and preach the gospel to all creation'" (Mark 16:15 NIV).

*God, please burden us all with the desire to spread the Good News of Jesus Christ to everyone. The people of all nations need to hear about Your love for them. Jesus sacrificed Himself as a gift to the world. Help us to share that gift to those around us and those on distant shores.*

# Roo

## Robin McNaueal

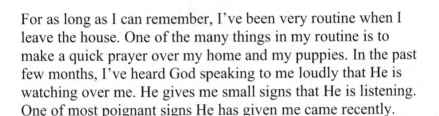

For as long as I can remember, I've been very routine when I leave the house. One of the many things in my routine is to make a quick prayer over my home and my puppies. In the past few months, I've heard God speaking to me loudly that He is watching over me. He gives me small signs that He is listening. One of most poignant signs He has given me came recently.

While leaving for work one day, my oldest dog (nicknamed Roo) was sick. I didn't think it was anything major. She had just thrown up. I thought nothing of it, cleaned it up and left. When I came home that night, she had again been sick. I had a vet appointment the next morning for another one of my dogs, and I made a mental decision to bring Roo as well. When the veterinarian staff worked her up, I mentioned that I'd felt a lump in one of her mammaes (breasts) a few months ago.

I explained that due to its nature, I thought it was probably just a cyst. They said they'd check it out. Later that afternoon, I received a call from the vet. Dr. Stacy told me that Roo was feeling better and the blood work was fine, but she had come back with markers for breast cancer! I was devastated! Roo has been with me for six and a half years, and she is my closest companion who has endured lots of changes while I've been living so far from home.

Dr Stacey recommended radical surgery, which included removing that breast, the adjoining one, and her adjacent lymph node, as well as spaying her. I agreed immediately, and the surgery was soon done. Roo bounced back wonderfully following her major surgery and has been blossoming under the added attention she's been receiving. I, on the other hand, have been having such a "why" attitude towards the whole affair. Why Roo? Why me?

I called my best friend who has been a big part of my Christian walk in the past few years. Tiffany said, "Sister, that's amazing!" Amazing? She went on to remind me that if Roo hadn't been sick the night before, I wouldn't have brought her in to the vet's office the next day and remembered to mention the lump I'd felt so many weeks before.

It may not have been diagnosed until her next bi-annual check-up. She said, "It's so God!" I felt God wink at me just then. I heard a song in my head that I hadn't heard in a long time: "I Will Never Forget You," by Carey Landry. God was once again shouting to me that He is watching over me!

"But Zion said, 'The LORD has forsaken me, the Lord has forgotten me.' 'Can a mother forget the baby at her breast and have no compassion on the child she has borne? Though she may forget, I will not forget you! See, I have engraved you on the palms of my hands; your walls are ever before me'" (Isaiah 49:14-16 NIV)

*Father, God, thank You for never forgetting me and for watching over me even when I don't realize it. Help me now to recognize all that You have done and are doing for me.*

# He Stripped Me of Sin

Felecia Clarke

I approached the prayer room at church before service started on Sunday to cleanse myself of iniquity. I was berating myself for a sin I'd committed just minutes before. Dropping my Bible and purse into a chair, I raised my hands up palms open to God and closed my eyes to receive His forgiveness.

I started to speak, but as I spoke my words sounded hollow and empty, as if I was just confessing to sound and act contrite. This realization caused me to stutter, and I stopped speaking. My stomach began to roil, and a desperate awareness washed over me of just how wicked I was.

Was I there to play-act a confession like an actor on a stage? Did I even mean what I was saying? My arms dropped dully to my sides, my head fell forward limp in sorrow, shame surrounded me, and tears fell from my eyes. Was there no depth to my sinful behavior? How could I come to the Father in such a state? Even my tears were subject to inspection.

But my tears were genuine. Real tears for a real God who I trusted to remove my sins....the ones I came in here to release to Him, and the sin I just committed in prayer. I am knocked to my knees by my absolute need for His grace and mercy.

I blinked back fresh tears as the Holy Spirit simultaneously convicted me and lifted my disgrace high, putting it in full view of the Heavens. With a deep breath I resumed my prayer and now my words were honest and sincere.

My heart poured out as I truly confessed and asked for forgiveness. Then in the quiet moments afterward, the prayer room clock softly ticked the minutes away, and my Lord God showered me with His grace and I was free again.

"See, I have removed your iniquity from you, and I will clothe you with rich robes" (Zechariah 3:4b NKJV).

*Lord, my heart swells with gratitude that I can stand before Your mercy seat. Though Satan attempts to hold my sin fast upon me, You remove it from me with a wave of Your almighty hand. Humbled am I to be filled with Your Spirit, and that I have found Your favor.*

# Peace During the Storm

## Stacey Tuley

When it came time that delivery was imminent, I was dilated to 6cm and I knew it wouldn't be long. It was now time for me to allow myself to visit my feelings of loss. I was scared. I didn't know what to expect. What was it going to be like to deliver a lifeless baby?

Would they let me hold her immediately like my previous deliveries? How would I deal with this? My husband and I named her Anna Catherine. As I think about her, I begin to cry and grieve, but God stops me in my tracks. I close my eyes and there I went for a chat with God.

He reminded me of how the disciples didn't understand Jesus when He talked about going somewhere the disciples couldn't follow, but they had to trust Him. I didn't understand why Anna had to go, but God asked me, "Do you trust me?"

I delivered Anna the Thursday before Good Friday in 2004. I felt in a mild sense like she was my sacrificial lamb. She had to die, so that I could live. God truly gave me His total peace that day. I knew that if I died, I was at peace with God. I used to work with moms in the neonatal nurseries at a hospital. Some of these moms gave up their babies for adoption.

Because of my work, I was able to see God as Anna's adoptive Parent and me as her birth parent. Somehow, it also gave me peace to think that God would raise her in a perfect place called Heaven. Yes, I did grieve, but God comforted me by reminding me that He was caring for Anna.

"Peace I leave with you; my peace I give you. I do not give to you as the world gives. Do not let your hearts be troubled and do not be afraid" (John 14:27 NIV).

*Dear God, only You can give us perfect peace that is incomprehensible. Only You can calm Your child in the midst of the storms of life. Thank You, for loving us so much that you meet us where we are in the midst of our grief, trepidation, and fear; and You faithfully fill us with Your peace. Lord, I know that the peace You gave me, You will give to others! Thank You, for the gift of Your perfect peace.*

# Picture Perfect Puzzle

### Tiffany Locke

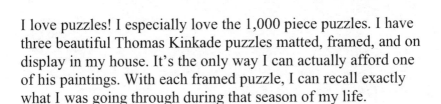

I love puzzles! I especially love the 1,000 piece puzzles. I have three beautiful Thomas Kinkade puzzles matted, framed, and on display in my house. It's the only way I can actually afford one of his paintings. With each framed puzzle, I can recall exactly what I was going through during that season of my life.

Each puzzle reminds me of the struggles I was experiencing and what I was doing to figure out the solutions. They are each like a personal testimony of my life. The last two months I've managed to work on two puzzles. I'm going thought a lot! Right now my life feels like a puzzle and God is holding all the pieces. They are hiding in his shirt pocket and He's only revealing to me one piece at a time.

When putting a puzzle together, I turn over all the pieces and make sure I have all the edges as I connect them. Then I start filling in the middle. This is kind of like what God does with each of us. He sets up boundaries (the edges) and then piece by piece He reveals to us the perfect picture that He has for us. As I sit at the kitchen table finding pieces that will form a beautiful picture and thinking about life, I sense God directing me and reminding me that He has all the pieces.

He is telling me that He is the artist. I just need to "be still." I've learned that with each piece He will reveal a new direction and a new awareness. Once again, I will hang on my wall reminders that He has all the pieces of my puzzling life. My hope is that when people look at my life after all the pieces are put together, the final picture will be of Jesus in all that I've done and all that He has done in me.

"'For I know the plans I have for you,' declares the LORD, 'plans to prosper you and not harm you, plans to give you hope and a future'" (Jeremiah 29:11 NIV).

*Father, at times I feel like I'm one jumbled mess. I'm so overwhelmed with the stresses of just being a wife, a mother, a daughter, and a friend. I know You have all the puzzle pieces of my life and You know what every day and hour is supposed to look like. Help me to be patient with the pieces that You have not shown me and help me to visualize the entire finished product through Your eyes.*

# What is Good

Susan Shipe

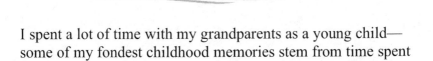

I spent a lot of time with my grandparents as a young child—some of my fondest childhood memories stem from time spent with them.

In 1959, the moments after accepting Jesus as my Savior, I ran to their house around the corner to tell them the good news! Now in reflection, as a Mimz' (Grandma) to two, I understand the elation they poured over me. There really is no greater joy than to hear that your children and grandchildren walk in Truth (3 John 4)!

However, as a teenager, I found Grandma far too old-fashioned, so I always came up with an excuse to not go to their house. As a young wife and mother, she seemed just a bit too conservative for my modern ways.

I look back and sorely regret not spending more time with her, and as time passed, I began to relish her knowledge and wisdom she imparted to me. Her patient endurance and her rock solid faith when Grandpa went home to Heaven has shaped my own faith. Her unwavering trust in God to give her peace in her last days succumbing to cancer, which took her life within 45 days, has shown me how to trust.

Grandma taught me "what is good." Over the years, and more so recently as I begin to mature into my 60-something's, the wisdom of my grandparents become more and more precious to me. I am now a grandmother to two almost adult kids, and I sense an urgency to teach them every possible life principle!

Our grands love being with us and we are blessed. Truth, in love, is critically important in a culture where anything goes. Everything doesn't go in God's economy, and it is imperative we teach those coming up behind us to discern what is good and what is not good. I'm honored to pass on what I've learned from my grandparents to future generations.

"Likewise, teach the older women to be reverent in the way they live, not to be slanderers or addicted to much wine, but to teach what is good" (Titus 2:3 NIV).

*Father God, I want to mature in You. I pray that You help me to grow into the image of Christ. I want to pass on my wisdom and faith, like my grandparents passed it on to me. Thank You for giving me a legacy grounded in what is good.*

# Immediate Praise

### Lindsey Plumleigh

Why is it so hard to praise God while angry, or frustrated, or scared? To be able to take a step out of the moment just to praise our Savior should be our go-to move. But when situations and circumstances consume us, we default to our raw emotions.

It is something I struggle with daily. Recently, my one-year-old son and I took a trip to the grocery store to pick up a few things for the week. I had spent time budgeting, sorting coupons, and even creating a list to make our trip more efficient.

It should have been a fast and easy haul. I was burning through the aisles, grabbing items and checking them off the list. Meanwhile, my son was becoming uneasy and was trying to squirm his way out of the buggy. I pushed through, handed him a teething ring, and continued grabbing items.

Soon, he began to cry and thrash his arms, so I picked him up and carried him in my arms. We continued on and made our way to the cashier for checkout. Waiting in line was torture. My left arm was now numb from carrying my son.

I was sorting through coupons with one hand and trying to find my debit card with my only finger left….my thumb. Somehow, we made it through checkout and headed to our car. I pulled the buggy alongside my car door and loaded my son into his car seat.

As I walked around the passenger side of my vehicle, I noticed my buggy was not there. Nope, it was taken by the biggest rush of wind. The buggy slammed right into the car parked across from me.

The buggy hit the car so hard, that it set off the car alarm. I froze and looked around to see if people were watching this chaos. I decided to grab my buggy, quickly load my car, and end this trip. When I got into my seat, I sat for a minute. I thought, *What would happen if I punched my steering wheel? Would the airbag pop in my face?*

Then, I felt anger turn into tears. I laid my head on the steering wheel and prayed. "God, I need you! I am angry and I need to hear you!" I turned on my radio to the local Christian channel and an awesome worship song was playing. I began mouthing the words, hoping this would calm me down.

Within minutes of praising and worshipping God in the grocery store parking lot, I began to feel at peace. My embarrassment quickly faded, my anger dissolved, and my patience was restored. I looked into the infant mirror hanging in the back seat and saw that my son was content and playing with his shoes. Why couldn't I have just praised God immediately?

"I will exalt you, my God the King; I will praise your name for ever and ever. Every day I will praise you and extol your name forever and ever. Great is the Lord and most worthy of praise; his greatness no one can fathom" (Psalm 145:1-3 NIV).

*Lord, You know my heart, and You feel my emotions. Please God, comfort me and give me peace to let this moment pass. Help me sing Your praises and worship You immediately when these feeling arise. I know that You are with me and I am never alone. Thank You for new mercy and restored focus.*

# Fruit of Obedience

Susan Wood

I was walking with my dog, Ashley, thinking about what a wonderful doggie life she has and how she experiences so much more freedom than other dogs.

Ashley is the smartest, most obedient dog I've ever known. She is with us everywhere we go. We have a traveling family business, so we can bring our dog to work. We travel in an RV for work trips, and Ashley enjoys the many habitats, landscapes and smells throughout the country.

At our home in the mountains of upstate New York, Ashley has her own doggie door and 14 acres at her disposal. She can freely come and go as she pleases. We can give her that privilege because Ashley always stays close to home and never wanders. With all her freedom, she has never strayed off our property.

We winter in Texas where I love to run and walk along the beach each day with Ashley. I don't need a leash because she always keeps pace with me. Wherever we are, I can walk her without a leash because she obeys my voice and always picks up her head to see where I am. She's keenly aware of me and keeps me in her sight. Even if she finds an interesting smell in the grass, she quickly flashes a glance to make sure I'm still there and she hasn't drifted off.

I am always on her mind. She safely trusts in me and knows I will always provide for all her needs. I was thinking about the freedom Ashley enjoys, and that her freedom is the very fruit of her obedience. I thought about how similar this is to my relationship with Jesus. The more obedient I am to Him, the more freedom I can enjoy.

In my life, walking by Jesus' side, I need to keep picking my head up to make sure He's still in sight and that I haven't wandered off. Even if there's something of great interest along my path, I need to keep flashing a glance, confirming that I am still near Him. I need to make sure that even with all the concerns of life that I am keenly aware of Him and that He is always on my mind.

"The LORD is my shepherd; I have all that I need. He lets me rest in green meadows; he leads me beside peaceful streams. He renews my strength. He guides me along right paths, bringing honor to his name" (Psalm 23:1-3 NLT).

*Father, help me to stay right by Your side. You have given me freedom because I safely trust You and Your ways. I want to always know that You will provide for all my needs. I will look to You for everything. I never want to stray, even if I have all the freedom in the world.*

# God's Box

## Cheryl Grundy

Unpacking recently after a move, I was delighted to find a box that a friend had given me a few years ago. It is a beautiful box. It is small, white, and elegantly decorated. The top has lace and a silk ribbon adorned with pearls. I thought she had made it especially for me until she announced that it was "God's Box."

Seeing the puzzled look on my face, she proceeded to explain. "This box is God's Box and any time you are worried about something or if you have something you want to give to God, just write it on a small slip of paper and put it in God's Box. There is just one Rule: Once you put it in God's Box, you cannot take it back out! In other words, give your worry to God and let Him take care of it...don't try to intervene and take it back. Let Him have it."

My friend knew me too well. She knew that I struggled with trying to be self-sufficient and independent. This box was her way of helping me to truly give my worries and petitions to God. I remember the first time I placed a slip of paper in the box. It wasn't very long before I wanted to open the box and take it out. I was reminded that if I took the slip of paper out, I was not trusting God with what was written upon it. I couldn't have it both ways.

Either I gave it to Him or I didn't. I either trusted Him with it or I didn't. Wow! What a realization I had through the symbolic example of the God's Box. I thank the Lord for the special friend who took the time to give me a wonderful gift that so beautifully signified giving my worries and petitions to the Lord and trusting Him with them.

Trust God in all things! He is Faithful!

"Rejoice in the Lord always. I will say it again: Rejoice! Let your gentleness be evident to all. The Lord is near. Do not be anxious about anything, but in everything, by prayer and petition, with thanksgiving, present your requests to God. And the peace of God, which transcends all understanding, will guard your hearts and your minds in Christ Jesus (Philippians 4: 4-7 NIV).

*Dear Lord, I thank You for Your faithfulness, Your promises, and Your love. I thank You for Christian friends. Help me learn to lay my burdens at Your feet and to trust You with all my heart. For without You, I can do nothing. Help me to be obedient to Your Word, to accept Your timing, and trust Your resolution.*

# Another Birthday

Vicki Beck

As my birthday approaches, I find myself (once again) considering my appearance. I notice more fine wrinkles on my hands and arms, and fine lines around my eyes. It seems like they crept there almost overnight. And now—unless I rinse L'Oreal medium golden-brown hair color into my hair every couple months—my gray hair becomes more obvious every day. Yikes … I still have a year before I hit the big "5-0!"

Our society places great importance on personal appearance. We must look young and beautiful—regardless of our age. Sometimes it's tough not measuring my appearance by those standards and remember instead that God finds more beauty in me with each passing year. He finds beauty in my heart and takes joy in watching me become the woman He designed me to be.

He is the great designer—molding and making me and you into a more beautiful creation with every breath we take. Although my body continues to change with each passing year and I don't plan to stop coloring my hair anytime soon, I'll celebrate each birthday with the knowledge that God sees beauty in each and every wrinkle and gray hair. And that's definitely something worth celebrating!

"Gray hair is a crown of splendor; it is attained by a righteous life" (Proverbs 16:31 NIV).

*Thank you, God, for another birthday. The days of my youth seem to pass quickly, but Your love for me never fails. Please help me not get too caught up in how I look, but instead let my heart be found pleasing to You.*

# The Value of One

Erica Skattebo

As I bent down to pick up the well-worn object while out walking, I was transported back to an elementary school yard playground in California. Toe-tempting, blonde-like sand covered every inch of the playground, including the spot beneath the slide where I found myself passing the time at recess. Kicking at the sand paid off…literally. Within a few minutes, I was "rich." Well, at least it seemed that way after finding a handful of mostly silver coins!

Finding money has always been exciting for me. It seems my two kiddos have caught the "coin craze" too. When a coin catches their eye, they nearly trip over each other while racing over to see who will get to it first. Though we occasionally find silver coins, it's more often that the copper ones are discovered while we are out and about.

What a story each coin must have, especially the pennies. We see the evidence of a hard life—dirty, bent, worn, scarred, and sometimes even broken. If only they could talk and tell us about the places they've traveled, the reasons for their "scars," the people they've met, and so on. Tip jars, junk drawers, drains, pockets, donation collection boxes, and maybe even the trash contain a high volume of these one cent coins. Why is that? In reality, those pennies have the lowest value. They aren't worthless, but are worth less. Those pennies can quickly be ignored, kicked, stepped on, or discarded with ease.

But picking up the penny that day instantly reminded me of this verse from God's Word: "Verily I say unto you, Inasmuch as ye have done it unto one of the least of these my brethren, ye have done it unto me" (Matthew 25:40b).

Like a penny, we all have a story too. There are well-worn, well-traveled, broken, and scarred people all around us. We've passed them at the street corner, walked by them the store, or even glanced their way in our own church or community. In God's reality, "the least of these" has the highest value.

Showing Christ's love, care, compassion, forgiveness, grace, mercy, patience, and more with them is equal to doing it to the very one Who deems us as valuable in Him. These "pennies" all around us don't need to be polished and smooth to be used. God can use them just as they are. It's up to us to notice them and pick them up right where they are.

"But I am poor and needy; yet the Lord thinketh upon me: thou art my help and my deliverer; make no tarrying, O my God" (Psalm 40:17 KJV).

*Heavenly Father, thank You for thinking about me even in my poor and needy condition. May I follow your example and value others the way You do. Give me eyes to see the needy, rather than myself, and show them the love of Jesus.*

# Held

## Christina Ketchum

I work as a Medical Social Worker for Driscoll Children's Hospital in the Neonate Intensive Care Unit (NICU). Like all jobs, mine involves tasks that are extremely challenging. One of the most challenging tasks is that I have to be present and assist with all infant deaths that occur in the NICU. This task has become increasingly more challenging since I became pregnant six months ago.

There are no magic words that I can say to stop the parents' pain and suffering. As I sit with them, I question why God would bless a family with a baby only to take him away three weeks later. It seems cruel. I have witnessed many infant deaths and have never been given the answer to this question. The one truth I hold to is that children are a blessing from God, but they are also His children.

God simply gives us the honor and privilege of loving and caring for His children during the time that He allows. God may bless us with a child that we take care of for 18 years only to release him into the world after high school. God may bless us with a special needs child that we have the honor of taking care of for his entire life. God may also bless us with a child that we are allowed to take care of and hold for only three weeks.

We have no control over God's timing. All we can do is decide what we will do with that precious time. So now when I sit with a family as they experience the loss of a child, I pray God gives them comfort and peace. I pray God gives them strength to accept His timing and to love their baby as much as possible until God takes him and holds him in His own arms.

"Blessed are those who mourn, for they will be comforted" (Matthew 5:4 NIV).

*Dear Lord, I know that I cannot always understand Your timing and Your will. Help me to trust Your decisions and faithfully walk through the tragedies life throws at me. Please comfort me and others during times of heartache, loss and sorrow.*

# Go Eat Popcorn

## Jeannie De La Garza

Around a year ago, I began hearing through some of my friends at church that a "ladies writing group" was putting some of their devotionals together. This group was getting ready to meet for the first time at the leader's home. The leader of the group was a published writer. My interest was piqued! So I gave her a call and got the information on where they were going to meet.

In my heart I have always known that sharing everything God has done in my life is the right thing to do—it reveals His glory. Writing devotionals seemed like it might be an appropriate way in which I could do this. However, I've never had a desire to share my testimony because I'm a private person by nature, and writing about my personal life and sharing with others was a scary idea.

This led to a dilemma: I can't show God's glory in my life if I'm not willing to share my life with others. At our first meeting, I was struck at how warm, kind and encouraging our leader was. She explained to us that we were "sharers" not simply "writers." She showed us several examples of devotionals to encourage us. I remember thinking, "I can do this! I can share some of the things that God has done for me!"

At our second meeting we were busy editing devotionals, looking up scripture, and enjoying Christian fellowship. Then, one of the women asked, "Where's Ephesians?" Still concentrating on reading, I said, "Go Eat Popcorn." I continued reading, but I noticed the entire room got very quiet.

Our leader said, "I think we have some popcorn."

I looked up and wondered what I had missed.

Then another woman said, "I may have some in my purse left over from the kids' movie today."

At this point the room was even quieter. Finally, the leader asked, "Would you like some popcorn?" I was surprised until I recalled my blurted out "words of wisdom." I started laughing so hard, which really broke the ice for me. I explained that "Go Eat Popcorn" is an acronym for the first several books of the Bible. One of my children had taught me this over twenty years ago, and I still use it today.

I was still laughing on my way home, and it dawned on me that I need to basically get over myself. It is not about me; it is about Him. I need to just share with others what God has done for me. Sharing God's glory is one of the ways I can show Him gratitude, while hopefully encouraging others as well. Many times the devotionals we write mean more to the reader than we can ever imagine. We just need to be willing to share!

"Therefore encourage one another and build each other up, just as in fact you are doing" (1 Thessalonians 5:11 NIV).

*Father, help me to get beyond my own insecurities and fears in order to share what You have accomplished in my life. I know that my life experiences can help others in their walk with You, and I'm ready to obey Your leading. God, please fill me with Your confidence so that I may share.*

# A Father's Eyes

Ann Cornelius

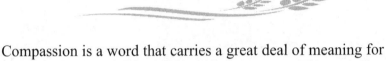

Compassion is a word that carries a great deal of meaning for the Christian. Jesus was a man of compassion. When people are hurting, they need the compassion of others. Do we have trouble seeing the needs of hurting people?

Sometimes a kind word, a gentle smile, or taking a casserole over to a hurting family demonstrates the love of God more emphatically than the best sermon in the world. It takes having our Father's eyes to see the needs of those around us.

As a teenager, my sister and I rode a bus every day to high school. There was a girl our age who had lost her mother to cancer. She wanted to hang around with us, but she was a little over weight and didn't dress very well. We really didn't want to be her friend. We were not unkind, but we didn't make any effort to befriend her.

After I graduated from high school, I went into nurses training. One of my rotations was to the San Antonio State Hospital. On my first day there, I saw this girl. She was a patient in the psychiatric hospital. Her presence really convicted me of my lack of compassion. What if my sister and I had befriended this girl? Would it have made a difference in her life?

We never know when an opportunity to share God's love and compassion will come our way, but we must be ready and willing to have our Father's eyes and take advantage of it.

"Finally, all of you, live in harmony with one another; be sympathetic, love as brothers, be compassionate and humble" (1 Peter 3:8 NIV).

*Dear God, open my eyes to the hurting people all around me. Help me to know how to meet their needs in a way that will demonstrate Christian love. Keep me from doing anything that would not reflect well on the family of God. Bring to my mind the people that You would like me to show compassion to.*

# The Power of Prayer

Tasha Schaded

My husband and I have been going through some difficult times financially since our move. I had started down a new career path, and he was finally getting back into the swing of things with his job. Then we found out we were going to have a baby. We were so excited!

Everything was going great until morning sickness kicked in all day. I was miserable and couldn't continue to work. That has hurt us badly. We were already living paycheck to paycheck, just barely covering our bills and living on credit for other necessities.

One payday, I was sitting down figuring out the bills and noticed we had exactly enough money to pay our bills if we didn't tithe. I became weak and decided to pay the bills without first talking to my husband. After telling him, he became upset that I wasn't strong enough with my faith to know that God would provide for us. There was nothing I could do about it now.

For the next two weeks, I kept hearing our pastor talk about tithing out of obedience and stealing from God. It was really weighing on me. When the next payday came around, I sat in front of my computer, prayed to the Lord for forgiveness for what I had done and asked him to help bless our financial situation.

This time I tithed first. Then, I went on to pay all our bills, and I realized that we still had money left over to live on. I thought, "Wow! He heard my prayer." That same day, I had a wonderful lady come clean my house since I have been so sick—it hadn't been cleaned in months.

She worked so hard all day and after she was done, I pulled out some cash to pay her and she wouldn't accept it. She told me that this was the first time ever that she felt the Lord telling her to clean for free. I argued with her to take the money because she had worked so hard, and I couldn't allow her to take no payment.

After all my trying to convince her to take my money, I gave in. I couldn't go against what she was saying was God's will for her. After all of this, I have still been praying and God has still been obviously answering my prayers. Prayer really is powerful!

"What other nation is so great as to have their gods near them the way the LORD our God is near us whenever we pray to him?" (Deuteronomy 4:7 NIV).

*Lord, I thank You that I can come straight to You, Father, with my needs and worries. I'm thankful that I have learned to listen when You speak to me with Your answers. Please continue to help me strengthen my faith and put all my trust in You.*

# Twine

## Christina Ketchum

For a long time, I believed that God was able to show His power tangibly to people but just not to me. I concluded that I wasn't on His radar, but I was totally okay with experiencing His power vicariously through others.

One day, I was taking my three small children around our neighborhood for a walk. My four and six-year-old were slowly riding their bikes, and I was pulling my two year old in a red wagon. I had to be very careful because our neighborhood does not have sidewalks, so we all had to use the street.

After about twenty minutes, my older two kids starting crying because their little legs were exhausted from pedaling their bikes on the street. My six-year-old son started speeding up towards the house and my four-year-old daughter started lagging behind. I was frantic because we were still about fifteen minutes away from the house.

I knew if I didn't get the situation under control, one of my kids might run towards a moving car, and I wouldn't be able to get them in time. I couldn't leave my two-year-old alone in the wagon to run after my other kids because he was also trying to get out.

I desperately wanted some type of string or rope. I knew I could tie the two bikes to the wagon, and I could pull all three kids home and ensure none of my kids ran out into traffic. My children started crying louder and running and speeding away from me, so I called out to God. I told Him to show Himself to me.

I knew He could do it. I've heard stories of Him showing His power to my friends and read about it in hundreds of books. I cried out to Him and said, "Please, just give me some twine or something!"

I walked a couple steps and looked down to see an entire spool of twine laying in the gutter of our neighborhood street. I couldn't believe it! God showed His power to me in a real way!

I picked up the spool and tied both bikes to the back of the wagon and proceeded to pull my three kids home. My older two kids were so happy not having to pedal their bikes, and I was happy to have control over the situation again.

But above all else, I was ecstatic that God showed Himself to me. I realized that God wants to show Himself to every single person, but we have to not set limits on His presence. We will never see what we refuse to believe. We must have faith that He loves us and wants to reveal Himself to us.

"I love the Lord, for he heard my voice; he heard my cry for mercy" (Psalm 116:1 NIV).

*God, thank You for hearing and answering my prayers. Help me to believe that You want to be a part of even the smallest details of my life. Give me ears and eyes to see Your movements all around me.*

# Faith or Fact

*Tammi Slavin*

I recently had a conversation with a dear friend about a topic that many Christians have to address. She was sharing her struggle in witnessing to a friend about Christ. She considered herself a "Baby Christian" and the person she was witnessing to was very set in his non-Christian belief system. He had grown up in a communist country, and he was (understandably) bitter about religion.

However, he did seem to want to engage her in debate over the shortcomings of Christians and theological conundrums in general. My friend was frustrated trying to answer his questions about the loving nature of God, about sin in the world, and other difficult topics.

Generally, theology is a topic that I get very excited about because I love researching the verifiable and historically accurate aspects of the Bible. I also love to apply logic and reason to conclude that Jehovah is the One True God, that Jesus Christ did die to atone for our sins, and that His resurrection was witnessed by many people.

My acceptance of salvation in Christ was by faith, but I have always been happy that I can prove certain aspects of Christianity. My friend shared her salvation story with me. She is a very logical type of person; but at one point in her life, she had to lay it all down and cry out to Jesus in faith. I could not stop thinking about our conversation because I could see how sincere and pure-hearted she was in her quest to help others believe in Christ.

I know that the one thing I cannot convince someone is to have that same heart-felt yearning. That night I looked up the Message translation of Hebrews 11:6, and I was blown away! It states, "It's impossible to please God apart from faith. And why? Because anyone who wants to approach God must believe both that He exists and that He cares enough to respond to those who seek Him."

Wow! Someone can be convinced that God is real and Jesus walked the earth; however, it's just not enough to be dazzled with facts! The seeker has to know that God is not a dispassionate deity, observing from his throne. God wants us to seek Him through faith. This is so humbling and beautiful to me. It made me realize that faith should be the starting point in sharing God with others, not logical debates.

"He made no distinction between us and them for he purified their hearts by faith" (Acts 15:9 NIV).

*Lord, forgive me where I may have fallen short in having the faith I need to please You. Help me to be sensitive to those who are searching for You. Let me be not only a source of information, but more importantly, an example of someone living out their salvation through faith and passion for You.*

# Sins of the Spirit

### Dixie Phillips

Lord, today I was angry. When friendship was extended, I responded coolly. I felt justified. After what she had said, I had a right to treat her that way. About whom does she think she is making such condescending statements? I haven't done anything to deserve her cruel comments.

In the long run my refusal of her friendship will teach her a valuable lesson: Her behavior is unacceptable. I will not reward such dysfunction. After all, her attitude is totally despicable, and it goes against the teachings in Your Word, Lord. I certainly don't want to enable her.

I've settled it once and for all. I am right! No doubt about it. There is no need in my discussing it any more. I am positively...positively...miserable! *"Why am I in such unrest, Lord? How is it possible that I can I be right and yet be so wrong?"*

In the depths of my soul, I discerned that I also am part of the problem. I am like the prodigal son's older brother who had a spiritual disease: He was angered by his father's mercy. Thank You, Holy Spirit, for giving me a much-needed diagnosis: I have sins of the spirit, a spiritual malady, which can render the patient unable to give love.

Many times spiritual manifestations can be masked and difficult to detect. The symptoms include polite coolness towards others, consumed with proving my point, a need to persuade others, and loving my opinions more than people.

But, if we are willing patients, the symptoms only last for a short time. The Holy Spirit gives the biblical antidote, so that the disease does not spread to vital organs.

"The older brother became angry and refused to go in. So his father went out and pleaded with him" (Luke 15:28 NIV).

*Lord, help me to love as You love today. Thank You for helping me forgive those who have hurt me. Forgive me, Lord, and help me to right my wrong. Life is too short for me to feed this grudge. Bring to my mind someone I need to forgive today.*

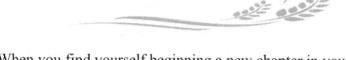

# New Beginnings

## Tiffany Molina

When you find yourself beginning a new chapter in your life, you feel both anxious and excited. It is hard to start over or begin it again. We challenge ourselves and doubt everything along the way.

I am beginning multiple new chapters in my life, so my anxiety, doubt, and excitement are even higher. Being a woman, a mother, and a wife, of course, makes all of this an even bigger deal. My mind can't help to wonder, *Why do I have to start over and begin again? Is this the plan, and if so why I did I not get it right the first time?*

My first new beginning was finding myself as a new Christian and bringing God into my life. My second new beginning was with my husband. We have reunited after a lengthy separation. My third new beginning is a new job in a new town. (Well, that's two new beginnings in one). To be able to do something new or even do it over is a great opportunity for anyone.

I am enthusiastic about embracing these journeys. After a lot of thinking and praying, I realize that it's not what went wrong but more so about how to make it better and permanent. I think God understand that we sometimes won't get His plans right the first time and these "beginnings" or "redos" are just about Him pulling us back into His plan because we were lost.

"This means that anyone who belongs to Christ has become a new person. The old life is gone; a new life has begun!" (2 Corinthians 5:17 NLT).

*God, help me with my new beginning. I want to stay on Your path and keep myself committed to Your will and Your timing in all areas of my life. I'm excited about what You will do in this new season of life.*

# Waterfall

Estella Smith

One night during my quiet time, I was pouring out my desire to know God's Word more deeply. I told God that I wanted to be like a wine bottle: when the cork is popped, the contents just flow out. That is what I was wanting, but God so gently whispered, "Think bigger! A wine bottle will soon be empty, but a waterfall is continuously flowing."

Wow! What an amazing vision. God always has such a bigger picture. God revealed that the waterfall represented His Never-Ending-Flowing-Word because water is needed for survival, just as we need His Word. Satisfied with such a beautiful thought, I prayed and went to bed.

The next morning I was awakened at 5am. Since I never get up that early, I immediately asked God what He desired of me. God preceded to expand my image of the waterfall. I envisioned the waterfall once again (the water representing God's Word). He showed me a waterfall that was not flowing; it looked as if a dam had been built.

All I could see was the exposed rock that should have been covered by flowing water. God then revealed an opening in the rock like a cavern. In the opening was a treasure. He said when we are not immersed in His Word, we leave ourselves vulnerable and open to attack. What God was showing me is that we need to cover our treasure in His Word, so that we are protected from the enemy who wants to steal, kill, and destroy.

God went on to show me a vision of a waterfall that was flowing, but there were breaks in the water where rocks were poking out. He said when Believers are covering themselves in the Word; but they have strong holds—unforgiveness, sin, addictions—they create a break in the flow. And through that break in the water, the enemy can enter our vulnerable places and steal our treasure.

So from this beautiful vision, I see we must cover ourselves in His Life-Giving-Word and confess sin, let go of unforgiveness, and cast down strongholds. We must consistently be covered by God's Word, so we do not expose ourselves to the enemy's attack. We are in a relationship with God! He has graciously provided the never-ending, pure and life-giving flow of His Word! All we have to do is stay in its protection.

"Then the angel showed me the river of the water of life, as clear as crystal, flowing from the throne of God and of the Lamb" (Revelations 22:1 NIV).

*Lord, thank You that You have provided us with Your life giving Word that can protect and cover us. I pray, Lord, that if there are any breaks or dams in Your protection around me, that You would reveal them to me right now. I want my waterfall to be overflowing. I want to confess any breaks in the flow.*

# Exercise

Deedee Sharon

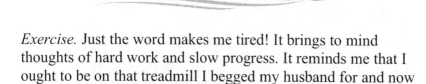

*Exercise.* Just the word makes me tired! It brings to mind thoughts of hard work and slow progress. It reminds me that I ought to be on that treadmill I begged my husband for and now serves as a "catch-all" in the corner of our bedroom. Unfortunately, my spirit is willing but my flesh is weak!

Isn't that the way it is with anything that is significant in our lives? It takes effort and discipline to maintain our physical health. Interestingly enough, it also takes effort and discipline to maintain our spiritual health. I know this to be true for myself, but I'm not the first to figure it out.

Paul tells us in 1Timothy 4:7 to "exercise yourself toward godliness." He figured out a long time ago that in order to be spiritually fit, there would need to be some hard work involved! We are not our own. We have been purchased, and do you know with what? Christ's life for ours....His life for mine and yours. Christ has paid the ultimate sacrifice for us; not so that we can waste away waiting for heaven to swallow us up, but so that we can serve Him.

He has a plan; and in order to be ready for the task, we must be fit! To put it simply, being spiritually fit requires a daily commitment to spending time in His word and spending time in

His presence. And there you have it— a fitness plan like no other with eternal rewards and benefits! If you miss a day or fall off the routine completely, just pick yourself up and get going again. Just make sure you get going!

"For physical training is of some value, but godliness has value for all things, holding promise for both the present life and the life to come" (1Timothy 4:8 NIV).

*Lord, I desire to be spiritually fit. I know that it requires great discipline, but I am certain that it is worth it! Help me to seek You every day and I pray for Your gentle nudge when I am tempted to deviate from the plan or give up.*

# Mine

## Monica Lugo

I took my precious guitar into the music shop to get looked at. It had taken a face-plant at church a few weeks ago while I was singing. All the guitar technician could say was, "It's bad, Monica, really bad."

I felt my heart twinge as never before. It appeared that what I thought was just a tumble was actually a "devastating blow."

Then I thought about life. Sometimes we think we have just taken a slight tumble only to look back and realize that we actually experienced a devastating blow, cracking our foundation. But God's Word says that nothing we do can separate us from His love.

No matter how far we tumble, He is always there to pick us back up. The guitar technician was able to fix my guitar. It will always have a character scar from the fall, but that makes the guitar mine.

It was at the moment when I received my guitar back, God reminded me that there is no crack that He is unable to repair. And when we will fall and take tumbles, He will be there every step of the way because we are His.

"But now, O Jacob, listen to the LORD who created you. O Israel, the one who formed you says, 'Do not be afraid, for I have ransomed you. I have called you by name; you are mine'" (Isaiah 43:1 NLT).

*Lord, thank You for accepting me for who I am—scars, flaws and all. I trust that You know me by name, and that You have claimed me as Your own. I pray that You take me under Your care and heal me when I tumble and fall.*

# Far From the Mark

### Kathy Cheek

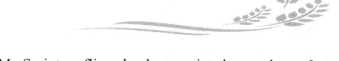

My Scripture flip calendar convicted me today as I read the daily verse: "But we all, with unveiled face, beholding as in a mirror the glory of the Lord, are being transformed into the same image from glory to glory, just as by the Spirit of the Lord" (2 Corinthians 3:18 NKJV).

I paused with the flip calendar still in my hand meditating on the words of this single verse and thought about the work God does to transform me to the image of His Son, Jesus.

Oh, I want to be transformed! I want to be more like Jesus. There are days I can attest to the fact this work is genuinely underway, and I know God is working on me and progress is being made on my part.

But today when I read that verse, all I could think was *I am so far from the mark of where I should be.*

I continue to stumble in areas where I know better or should know better by now. I am re-learning lessons long learned but I regress. Will I ever keep my tongue under guard as I should? Why can't my propensity to form quick and erroneous assumptions just stop? When will my heart naturally overflow with love to everyone? Yes, even the ones we find hard to love.

I had to stop making this mental list of all my shortcomings and remind myself hope is not lost. God is working on me. That does not mean I will not have battles and struggles, but it does mean that if I offer myself to Him to actively work in my life, I will be changed. I will be transformed from glory to glory.

"I beseech you therefore, brethren, by the mercies of God, that you present your bodies a living sacrifice, holy, acceptable to God, which is your reasonable service. And do not be conformed to this world, but be transformed by the renewing of your mind, that you may prove what is that good and acceptable and perfect will of God" (Romans 12:1-2 NKJV).

*Father, thank You for changing me little by little into the image of Your Son. I am not perfect, but I know You are doing a good work in me. Help me to extend grace to myself even when I stumble sometimes. Let me focus on how much I have grown in Your Truth instead of my shortcomings.*

# Sunsets and Light Switches

Erica Skattebo

Perhaps one of my favorite sights to behold is a sunset. As the sky transforms into an ombre of oranges and pinks, the beauty is breathtaking. Slowly the sun disappears into the horizon while the clouds begin absorbing the melting beauty, illuminating the sky for just a bit longer. As time passes, night falls and my eyes begin to adjust to the darkness. Some of my favorite beachy things like birds, boats, and shells, that were once in clear view, now blend into the darkening sky, and I find myself blinking frequently to find them again.

Now focused on the sound, not the sight, of the crashing waves, I discover that I quickly get used to the rhythm and find it comforting. Comfort also comes in holding the hand of my husband who brought us to this place to celebrate our twenty-third anniversary. We enjoy the slow fade of sunset together.

Comfort seems far from reach, however, when I'm in a brightly-lit room at night and suddenly find myself in pitch-dark surroundings because someone pushed the light switch to the down position. Normally I am not scared of the dark, but if in unfamiliar territory, finding my way around in a dark room can lead to bruises, uncertainty, and sometimes even an overwhelming sense of panic. There is no advance warning to prepare. Just instant darkness from a turned-down light switch.

111

Watching your children grow up and leave the home, an endless struggling marriage, a consistent dwindling of the bank account, getting older and losing mobility—these are the slow fades of a sunset.

A house fire, terminal brain tumor, a stillborn baby, divorce, loss of a job—these are the instant darkness of a light switch.

Right now you may find yourself walking along the "beach of life" experiencing and adjusting to a gradual sunset or groping for someone or something in your sudden darkness. Jesus is the Light. Hold His hand and follow Him. He will bring a new sunrise, and He will turn on that light switch.

"And he shall be as the light of the morning, when the sun riseth, even a morning without clouds; as the tender grass springing out of the earth by clear shining after rain" (2 Samuel 23:4 KJV).

*Father, I've experienced sunsets and light switches of life, and I know that others, too, have or will experience them. Please help all of us to see Your light, follow it, and grow in our knowledge of Your glory so that through our sunsets and light switches, Your light will shine bright in us.*

# Godly Coffee

DeeDee Sharon

Recently, I attended a very special prayer breakfast. I was invited to pray with some of the most precious women of God while we shared a cup of coffee. I'm not a coffee drinker, so I was at a bit of a loss. All of the prayer warriors had mugs of a sweet-smelling Hawaiian brew, so I decided to give it a try. If this is what godly women did, I must participate!

We eventually moved to the living room, stood in a circle, held hands and began praying. Their hearts opened up and spilled out praises and petitions before the Lord, and I was humbled. These were truly rare gems that God was using for His glory. They sent me home with a mug and told me that every morning while drinking my Cup of Joe, I would be reminded to pray for them. And they would be doing the same for me.

For the next five days, I craved coffee. I kept dismissing it as a silly notion but soon gave up. I stopped by Wal-Mart on the way home from a friend's house. I bought coffee, creamer and filters hoping I would be able to figure out the process when I got home. I drank it (in my special cup) and no, it still did not taste good. My sinuses opened up and my eyes began to tear, but my taste buds were not appeased.

But as I sat drinking my java, I had a thought. Maybe the craving wasn't for the coffee as much as it was for the conversation with God. My mug was a symbol of the sweet prayers that were going up on my behalf and God was calling me to respond....to take a moment to sit down and just be with Him. I thank God for my coffee-drinking prayer buddies and for their example of faithfulness.

And I pray that I never lose my craving for the rich blend of warm fellowship with friends and sweet conversation with the Lord....coffee or no coffee.

"We ought always to thank God for you, [sisters], and rightly so, because your faith is growing more and more, and the love every one of you has for each other is increasing" (2 Thessalonians 1:3 NIV).

*Lord, I am blessed to have Christian friends in my life that pray for me. Thank You for their example of faithfulness that comes from time spent with You. Help me to remember that fellowship with You and fellowship with others is a sweet gift that should never be taken for granted. Your Word tells us that we are to "share one another's burdens," so right now I lift up my family and friends.*

# Creating Heritage

Tiffany Locke

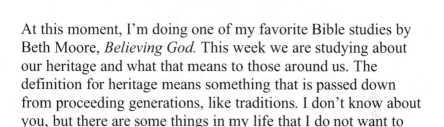

At this moment, I'm doing one of my favorite Bible studies by Beth Moore, *Believing God.* This week we are studying about our heritage and what that means to those around us. The definition for heritage means something that is passed down from proceeding generations, like traditions. I don't know about you, but there are some things in my life that I do not want to pass down to my children: my temper, my stubbornness, my teenage rebellion. Yikes!

The thought of passing those down to my children scares me to death. But there is hope! I can start a new heritage for my family, and so can you. I have special traditions that I would like to pass down to my children. I already see little things that they do, such as journaling and writing and highlighting in their Bibles, that they learned from me.

I see them becoming givers and encouragers, much like how my grandmother was in during her life. She was a remarkable woman. She loved the Lord and gave so much of herself to others, and I remember her Bible being full of prayer requests and answered prayers. I'm not sure where her Bible is today, but I would love to see it again and pass it down to my children.

My grandmother left a heritage of faith, encouragement, love and forgiveness. I didn't see it at the time, but now I do. I see what she left me and in return I'm passing it down to my children. My prayer is that when I go home to be with God, that my children and grandchildren can look at my life and my Bible and see all my highlights and written prayers and know that God is good and faithful.

"'You are my witnesses,' declares the Lord, 'and my servant whom I have chosen, so that you may know and believe me and understand that I am he. Before me no god was formed, nor will there be one after me'" (Isaiah 43:10 NIV).

*Lord, today help me create a godly heritage for my children and their children. I don't want them to come to me and ask why I did not tell them about Your love and faithfulness. I want them to see You through me. Let me start creating my heritage today.*

# Choosing Joy

### Bernadine Zimmerman

She lived a few houses down from me. She was often outside working in her yard or sitting on her front porch reading. We'd wave when I drove by and sometimes I'd pull over, and we would chat for a few minutes. One thing I noticed during the years we shared the same neighborhood was that she was always smiling.

It was after I came home from a short vacation that I realized I hadn't seen her in a while. I asked another neighbor if she'd seen her recently. It was then I learned that my neighbor had moved. She had lost her house to foreclosure. I was shocked. She always seemed so happy, and I couldn't believe what she had been dealing with in secret.

A few weeks later, I went grocery shopping when I heard someone calling my name. It was my old neighbor waving wildly at me and beaming her signature smile. I happily went over and hugged her. I told her how sorry I was that she had lost her home. I also mentioned that I never would have guessed she was dealing with something of that magnitude because she always seemed so happy. Her reply lingered with me. She told me that she'd known for some months that it was going to happen. There was nothing she could do to stop it, so she decided to enjoy the time she had left in her home.

She described her apartment, the place she now calls home, and explained how she had decorated it. Now her new home is her sanctuary. She talked with the same joy and enthusiasm that she displayed when we'd chat outside her house. She was still filled with joy despite her huge loss. In the face of something that could cause bitterness and despair she chose to be joyful. She had true inner joy.

It's so easy to get bitter—to drown in self-pity and regret when life becomes difficult and it seems as if everything is going wrong. However, my neighbor showed by her actions that she believes that even in the difficult times, God is always good and worthy to be praised.

"I pray that God, the source of hope, will fill you completely with joy and peace because you trust in him. Then you will overflow with confident hope through the power of the Holy Spirit" (Romans 15:13 NLT).

*Father, help me to be filled with the inner joy that comes from knowing and loving You. I don't want my peace and happiness to be dependent on my circumstances. I want to be an example of peace that surpasses all understanding to those who have their confident hope in You.*

# He Cares for You

### Joan Hall

While driving to Bible study, I cried out to the Lord, "Don't you care?" A few days earlier, my husband had chest pains and went to the emergency room. The pain was due to gastrointestinal problems, and he was able to return home.

However, we had to pay the hospital bill. Two years prior, John lost his job and health insurance. With his history of cancer, obtaining coverage wasn't easy. He found employment, but no benefits. For two years, I prayed that God would provide him with insurance.

*He doesn't care,* I thought. *If He did, He would have already answered my prayer. If God promises to meet all our needs, why has He not provided for this?* I glanced over at my study book, Jennifer Rothschild's *Walking by Faith – Lessons Learned in the Dark.*

How could I attend a Bible study, talk to others about faith, and still doubt God? Of all the scriptures containing affirmation of His love and care, the Lord brought to my mind Jesus' words found in Matthew 10:29-31: "Are not two sparrows sold for a penny? And not one of them will fall to the ground apart from your Father. But even the hairs of your head are all numbered.

Fear not, therefore; you are of more value than many sparrows" (ESV).

I repented of my doubt and anger. If God cares about the little sparrows, without a doubt He cares for His Children. I arrived at my friend's house with a lighter heart. When I stepped onto her porch, I saw a small bird resting near the front door. It was not there when another friend arrived moments earlier.

I knew God placed the little bird as a confirmation of His love for me. He provided a way to pay the hospital bill. Through that experience, I learned to trust Jehovah-Jireh. Today, John has a different job with insurance. God answered my prayer.

"Humble yourselves, therefore, under God's mighty hand, that He may lift you up in due time. Cast all your anxiety on him because He cares for you" (1 Peter 5:6-7 NIV).

*Lord, You are faithful and just. Forgive me when I doubt. Help me to see the valley times as a time of spiritual growth. Your Word is true, and You work all things together for good to those who are called to Your purpose.*

# Face to Face

## Holly Smith

Every time I sing it, I cry with strong emotion: "Turn your eyes upon Jesus. Look full in His wonderful face. And the things of earth will grow strangely dim in the light of His glory and grace." It's true.

It's amazing the perspective we gain in His Presence. It's the perspective that lightens our pathway and shows us that He is for us. Within that place, we can make choices. We can say "Yes" to the things that we know are His best. We can say "no" to the things that we are completely able to do, even gifted at, but it isn't His best.

In that place face-to-face, we come to know and discern. We aren't pleasing anyone or trying to earn awards for how good we are, but only living to please the Lord.

Years ago, I always said yes. It was to be accepted, earn favor, gain approval and because I didn't understand that "no" was an acceptable answer. So, I said yes. It wore me out. I began to despise some of the things I was doing, mainly because they weren't the right choices. Someone else was supposed to say yes.

But it filled my cup—my need for approval, my desire to be noticed. I wasn't full at all. Rather, I needed a timely word of course correction.

One day I heard a teacher say that "no" could be my default answer. I could say no all the time instead of yes. I could even say, *Let me pray about it.* But never again, unless I was certain, did I immediately answer yes. In those certain times, I went to the Lord in my heart and asked Him, "Best?" When He said yes, I said yes.

In this line, I said no to an event with God's leading—and it surprised me! I thought that maybe finances were the issue or even my tendency to avoid being part of a group. I'm not a groupie for anyone but Christ. I'm not shaped for that hole. I'm shaped to fit into the hole God has made for me—among whomever He brings for whatever time He ordains it. Jesus alone fits into the hole of my need. There's freedom in that.

I can say no. I can go or not go. But it's in the place of face-to-face that *I know*—hearing a voice behind me saying, "This is the way walk in it" (Isaiah 30:21). Daily you'll find me running to seek Him. It is something I say "yes" to and need so much, letting the things of this world grow dim in the light of Jesus' beautiful face.

"Trust GOD from the bottom of your heart; don't try to figure out everything on your own. Listen for GOD's voice in everything you do, everywhere you go; he's the one who will keep you on track" (Proverbs 3:5-6 MSG).

*Father God, I want to always seek You face-to-face, so I can be sure that I say yes to the right things and no to the wrong things. I want to live in the peaceful balance that You have for me. I don't want anyone's approval but Yours.*

# A Gift of Hope

### Laura Campise

*Hope.* It is a small word, but its power is amazing. After trying to conceive for six years, all that was left in me was a small ember of hope in my heart. With every negative pregnancy test, I would cry and turn to God in pain. He would comfort me with His words and promises; and like adding kindling to a fire, I was strengthened to try again.

After numerous tests, surgeries on both my husband's and my part, and medications that played havoc with my body and emotions, I was exhausted. Many times I felt just like someone running an uphill marathon in a mudslide. It seemed impossible. When I had a very early miscarriage, my husband and I were devastated. I spent lonely hours crying and in mourning, but I knew I had a choice. I could become negative and bitter, or I could hold onto God's promises and the hope that they give.

I have learned that hope was an action, and I had to choose to believe God's promises. After taking a break from fertility treatments, we decided to try again. I can't fully express how scared I was not only of failure, but also that my hope would die. It took us over six years to have our son, but I praise God every day for the strength He gave me. Today, as I look at my wonderful nine month old baby, I see the ember of hope realized, and it is beautiful!

"Hope deferred makes the heart sick, but a longing fulfilled is a tree of life" (Proverbs 13:12 NIV).

*Father, help me to learn to completely trust in Your word. Help me to have patience to wait for the fulfillment of Your promises. You know my heart best. Help me to hope in You for these needs.*

# *Ready Bride?*

Lynn Mosher

He shuffled his feet and wiped his sweaty palms on his jacket. His face twitched, producing a peculiar, cockeyed smile. Then, the bride began her promenade down the aisle, and the groom's whole body radiated with delight. They were so anxious to look their best for each other.

All decked out in their wedding finery, he was fit to meet his bride, and she fit to meet her bridegroom. As I sat in the chapel praying for them, the thought occurred to me: *Jesus is fit and ready to meet me as His Bride, but am I fit and ready to meet Him as my Bridegroom?*

If Jesus died so the Church, His bride, might be "without spot or wrinkle or any other defect—holy and unblemished" (Ephesians 5:27a Weymouth), then, as part of His Bride, how am I dressed? When the heavenly Bridegroom arrives, will I be garbed in an old rag, spotted with worldly residue? Or will I be "a bride beautifully dressed for her husband" in a spotless gown of holiness (Revelation 21:2 NIV)?

What am I doing to keep myself pure and holy and ready to have my Bridegroom carry me across that heavenly threshold? Will He radiate with delight in me, His bride? I want to be ready for when I meet Him face-to-face. I want to be like a giddy bride awaiting her bridegroom.

"Be dressed for service and keep your lamps burning, as though you were waiting for your master to return from the wedding feast. Then you will be ready to open the door and let him in the moment he arrives and knocks" (Luke 12:36-36 NLT).

*Lord, You loved me enough to die for me, to give me a pure wedding garment of holiness. May I love You enough to keep that gown unsullied from the world and meet You in holiness on Your return. May I be continually dressed and ready to go at a moment's notice.*

# My Heart Belongs to You

Angelica Estrada

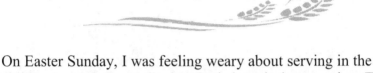

On Easter Sunday, I was feeling weary about serving in the children's ministry. I talked to God about it that morning. Then, I opened my Bible, and in my assigned reading for the day, I read the verse above Mark 9.37: "Whoever welcomes one of these little children in my name welcomes me; and whoever welcomes me does not welcome me but the one who sent me" (NIV).

God told me through this verse to keep doing it. So I did, but my heart wasn't in it. I was doing it out of obedience. I went to church. I served. I went to service. It was a great message. At the end of service, I witnessed many people give their hearts to Jesus. I heard a voice in my head asking, "How many of these people were able to give their undivided attention to the pastor's sermon because they didn't have to worry about their children disturbing service?"

It was awesome! God revealed to me one of the reasons why I have to serve. Finally, the service was over and it was time to get my five-year-old son from class. I picked him up and as soon as he walked out of the classroom, he said, "Mommy, did you know that Jesus died on the cross for you and me? And now we can go to heaven!"

It took everything in me not to cry—a joyful cry, of course! So needless to say, I was totally convicted from that day on. I want to ensure that my heart is in it a hundred percent. We serve for the kingdom of God, and God promises to bless us!

"But seek first his kingdom and his righteousness, and all these things will be given to you as well" (Matthew 6:33 NIV).

*Lord, thank You for using me to grow Your kingdom. I pray that You bless the faithful leaders who volunteer at church every Sunday. Continue to give them strength to do Your will. Please help me be obedient in serving in every area of my life.*

# Climbing Mountains

A.J. Pattengill

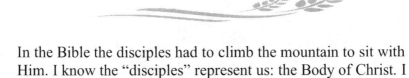

In the Bible the disciples had to climb the mountain to sit with Him. I know the "disciples" represent us: the Body of Christ. I understand that a Christian life is not a solo life. It's a community, as we fellowship, we worship, pray and encourage each other.

I had to climb my mountain by leaving America. I got on a plane to Guatemala, so I could find Jesus and sit with Him and the other disciples. Jesus began to teach us throughout our week-long mission trip. Each one of us had different experiences.

My experience occurred on the second day of our mission trip. We were visiting the poorest areas of Guatemala City, and there was a massive landfill with toxic dump. The trash site was so ghastly and smelled so bad that it was difficult for me to breathe.

In order to see this landfill, we had to go through a gravesite located on the edge of one of the mountains. I knew we were getting close to the end of the cemetery when we saw hundreds of vultures flying around the area. These nasty vultures were sitting on gravestones, watching and looking for something they could devour.

When we got out of the van by the edge of the mountain, we could see the bottom of the entire landfill. I was so shocked by how large the area was. It was about ten football fields. You could see people and children down there scavenging. They were hoping to find something valuable, so they could sell it. Also, there were many tents, so they could continue working through the night.

I looked up from where I was standing, and the area beyond and around the dumpsite was beautiful. Jesus spoke to my spirit, saying:

*You see such beauty all around? Our Father created the mountains, the lush green trees, the beautiful flowers, and the blue skies. What beautiful country. But then you look down there and you see the horrible toxic landfill. What our Father made was supposed to be for good.*

*When Our Father made His children, He saw all that He has made, and it was very good. Our Father in Heaven sees us now and He is so sad. He looks into His children that He made for good—like this beautiful country—but, instead of seeing good, He sees the toxic landfill filling up in the bottom of our hearts. It's so disgusting, and it deeply saddens Our Father. Even we Christians have toxic things in our hearts, and we can start to stink the atmosphere.*

Jesus put in my mind about the next warning, as I turned my head around to look at the vultures. These vultures are the demonic spirits that roam around into our toxic hearts to scavenge and devour us and take us to the grave and bury us. I knew what Jesus wanted me to do—to be His hands, His feet and His voice. I will speak and teach about Jesus and reach out to the hurt, the broken, and lost.

"One day as he saw the crowds gathering, Jesus went up on the mountainside and sat down. His disciples gathered around him, and he began to teach them" (Matthew 5:1-2 NLT).

*I am forever at Your will, Father. Send me wherever You would like me to go, so I can bring a message of warning and healing to Your people. Show me any toxic dump areas in my heart and destroy any vultures scavenging my soul.*

# In His Time

### Jennifer Keller

God has a will for each and every one of us, and it's on His time table. When I first met my husband, he didn't know who God was, nor did he know God's grace. He was one of those people who acknowledged that there was a higher power, but he didn't have a clue what that meant. At this time, I was what we call a "Baby Christian."

I myself was just learning about the mercy of God and how beautiful He really is. As I grew closer to God, I began to study His Word. I started to become frantic. I realized that I was starting to fall in love with a man who did not know Christ. We were not equally-yoked.

I know that God wanted me to marry a Christian. I knew that this man I loved needed to know God, and he needed to meet Him soon. As anxious as I was, I began to forcefully push Christ on him. I wanted him to go to church, to pray, read the Bible and to accept Christ as his Savior. I was desperate. Every day, I asked him to do at least one of those things.

The more I forced it upon him, the more he pushed the issue of salvation away. I couldn't understand why he wouldn't become a Christian for me? After nagging him for a couple of months, I realized that I couldn't keep on forcing God on him. The only thing I was doing was annoying him. At this point, I gave it to God with all my heart.

I loved this man and wanted to marry him. I wanted him to know Christ. I prayed every day for a long seven months that God would reveal Himself to him. The more I prayed, the more secure I felt that God would answer my prayer. One day, my boyfriend came home from work and began to ask some questions about God.

He said that God was showing him things about his life that could not be coincidental. I knew by the glow in his eyes that God had revealed Himself. My boyfriend saw signs that only he and God knew about. Wow! Look at what prayer did. Prayer saved a soul. I am so glad I gave the man I love up in prayer and allowed God to do the rest. I know that I will see my husband in heaven.

"So I say to you: Ask and it will be given to you; seek and you will find; knock and the door will be opened to you" (Luke 11:9 NIV).

*Dear Lord, I praise You for answering my prayers. Please help me to stay patient while I wait on Your will. I pray that I don't grow weary of prayer and that I remember to pray for everyone and everything.*

# I Have Purpose

Alene Snodgrass

I remember so many days when I'd sit and cry out to God, *Do I really have a purpose?* It seemed my life was all about wiping noses, running carpools and doing laundry. While being a full-time wife and mother of three children, there were many days I questioned myself. After a very challenging day in Mommyland, I had a "Calgon, take me away" moment.

I sat in my bathtub full of soothing bubbles asking God, *Why?* I admit—I was having a full-blown pity party right there in my own tub! Before I went to bed that night, I picked up my Bible and began to read. I had questions, and I needed answers.

God quickly led me to a verse that changed my heart. "So here's what I want you to do, God helping you: Take your everyday, ordinary life—your sleeping, eating, going-to-work, and walking-around life—and place it before God as an offering. Embracing what God does for you is the best thing you can do for Him" (Romans 12:1 MSG).

Unbelievable! God spoke right there: "It is in the ordinary, I find the extraordinary." It was my ordinary life I was questioning, because I was bogged down in the ordinary duties of being a mom and wife. Yet, God was saying to give Him the ordinary as an offering! I had wasted so much time and energy thinking I

135

wasn't useful because I didn't have what seemed an important job.

I hadn't stopped to realize that what I was doing was important. Yes, it might have been ordinary, but it was extremely important. Hallelujah! God crushed my insecurities that day with His message! I realized surrendering my ordinary life as an offering was my purpose. My sleeping, eating, wiping runny noses, changing diapers, doing laundry, running carpools, cooking and all those other daily chores now had meaning. They were an offering to God. Yes, I have a purpose!

"Her children stand and bless her. Her husband praises her" (Proverbs 31:28 NLT).

*Lord, please help me see Your purpose and extraordinary in the ordinary. May I learn to find fulfillment in the most mundane of tasks, because my eyes are fixed on you. Lord, I lift every moment and chore up to You as an offering.*

# Beautiful Weeds

Kerry Johnson

We were driving along US 301 one sunny spring morning when my son, Cole, commented, "Those are really tall, pretty flowers."

Construction crews had just paved a large sidewalk next to the road and no one had mowed the tall grass alongside it yet. Recent heavy rain and the constant Florida sunshine lent a beautiful, healthy flourish to all the vegetation.

I glanced toward the flowers and frowned in surprise. Instead of flowers, I saw wave after wave of tall, spindly weeds growing along the road, reaching over the new sidewalk. I commented back to him, "Those are actually weeds."

He was quiet for a moment then said, "But they look like flowers. They have bright colors and everything."

I briefly explained that weeds do sometimes have bright colors, but they choke out the real flowers and take over, blocking sunlight and soaking up moisture. Weeds are typically very hardy and some even have spiky protection on their leaves and stems.

Just like those colorful, overgrown weeds, sin always looks attractive. That's why we're tempted. Sin doesn't seem like it would hurt or that it has the power to take over our life, but it does, and it will.

Satan cleverly masks what can easily consume us in beautiful, tempting packages. Our selfish human nature is drawn to things and people who promise to help us, give us something, or make us feel good. Ultimately sin will cause decay in our soul and separate us from God. What a blessing that God's Holy Word is the best weed killer on the market!

The Bible provides warning and guidance for how to avoid sin. Most importantly, those who are in Christ Jesus are no longer slaves to sin. Christ-followers have the righteousness of our wonderful Savior and the power of the Holy Spirit within. We're given new eyes to discern the weeds of life from the beautiful roses of blessing God offers to His children.

"There is therefore now no condemnation to those who are in Christ Jesus, who do not walk according to the flesh, but according to the Spirit. For the law of the Spirit of life in Christ Jesus has made me free from the law of sin and death" (Romans 8:1-2 NKJV).

*Loving Father, thank You for the new life You give through faith in Your perfect Son, Jesus. Help us to live and breathe Your Word, and humble our hearts so we hear the Holy Spirit's voice and guidance. Remind us that no sin is worth the cost, and please give us strength to live Your truth each day.*

# A Mom's Identity

### Kimberly Dawn Rempel

"Are you afraid of losing yourself in motherhood?" she asks as I cry. I nod. "Who are you?" she asks.

Tears stream down my face as I search for an answer. I have no answer. The question rolls around in my head for days. *Who am I? What is identity*? I know what I do. I know my relationship to other people. I know my spiritual gifts. I know my personality. *So who am I? Who does God say I am?*

I am righteous through Christ, redeemed, secure, filled with the Holy Spirit, blameless in God's sight and saved. I have access to the Fruits of the Spirit (patience, love, and kindness), and I have boldness and power. I am a child of the Most High King. None of these things will be drowned by or lost in circumstance. My relationships, spiritual gifts and personality will not become lost in motherhood.

Quite the opposite—through being a mom I'll grow closer to Christ, closer to my children, and will grow a rich inheritance of faith, hope and love for generations. Suddenly, all the achievements, knowledge, experience and goals I'd hoped for do not matter. This task—this inheritance that will last for generations and impact eternity—is forever.

All of the sudden, the cleanliness of my bathroom doesn't matter. Whether my kitchen floor gleams or not is inconsequential. The stains on my stove are unimportant.

C'mon kids! Jump on the bed while I empty the clean-laundry basket on you. C'mon! Let's mop the floor together. Come work in my office with me! It'll be messy, take way too long and may not get done properly, but we're going to make great memories and build a strong foundation of love. I finally embrace what has eternal value!

"Open my eyes to see the wonderful truths in your instructions" (Psalm 119:18 NLT).

*Lord, help me to value things according to Your priorities. Help me to know what has eternal value and then focus only on those things. Lord, my housework is not the reason for my existence. I was created for You. Help me to walk in the purpose for which You created me. You have a wonderful plan for me. Thank You for that. I pray You open my eyes to what's eternal and help me to fix my eyes on You and Your mission for me.*

# In Case of Emergency

Erica Skattebo

The three numbers rolled off their tongues like water off a duck's back. "9-1-1," my kiddos chorused together after being asked what number to call if something happened to me while we were out on our morning walk. Of course, my goal isn't to scare them or talk doom and gloom, but to prepare them for what to do just in case. Family emergency preparedness speeches—you know how they go. At strategic (and even random) times they hear little safety tidbits like "Don't talk to strangers," "If you are lost, look for…," "If someone tries to…," "Stop, drop, and roll," and so on.

Now that the kids are in school, I find myself walking alone. More than once I have wondered what would happen should I have a medical (or other) emergency without them. What would I do? Would I be able to dial those well-known numbers? Would I panic or remain calm? Would I do exactly the right thing as the emergency unfolded?

Answers are easy to come by these days, aren't they? I often hear these phrases from not only adults, but kids as well: "Let me check my phone," "We can Google it," "Just look it up on the computer," "Let's check with so-and-so," etc. Turning to those things might be easy, but doing so is not always the best.

As I thought about that, my heart was pricked. Will they be ready when they find themselves alone? Have I taught (and am I teaching) my kids what to do in a real, this-is-what-really-matters emergency? A crisis of faith? Conflict? Friendships? Anger? Doubt? Fear? Disappointments? Trials? Am I teaching my kids to look for the easiest answers or the perfect ones? Sharing from personal experience is so easy, and yet...

"And that *from a child* thou hast known the holy scriptures, which *are able to make thee wise unto salvation* through faith which is in Christ Jesus. All scripture is given by inspiration of God, and *is profitable* for doctrine, for reproof, for correction, for instruction in righteousness: That the man of God may be perfect, thoroughly furnished unto all good works" (2 Tim. 3:15-17 KJV).

God knows how to take multiple calls at once and knows how to handle each one. He can identify the caller immediately and has endless resources. He is comfortable talking to people in various emotional states and knows exactly where to find us. He knows how to effectively listen and knows all the details (even before we do). The best part—God will always give the right answer to life's questions and emergencies. And the truth is, we can call on Him always, not just in emergencies. His Word, the Bible, is always available to us.

"Evening, and morning, and at noon, will I pray, and cry aloud: and he shall hear my voice" (Psalm 55:17 KJV).

*Lord, may I remember, remind, represent (model), and rejoice in Your divine power in all circumstances, big or small. It's in knowing You that I will be equipped for life and its emergencies.*

*Help me to direct my children to You for answers to all of their questions and emergencies in life.*

# Rock Star

## DeeDee Sharon

I was leading worship not long ago and we were about to sing one of my favorite songs. The band had an awesome intro and we had the congregation up on their feet clapping and about to blow the roof off the place. The crowd was pumped, and we hadn't even started singing yet! The energy was amazing!

The drums were pounding, the bass was vibrating in my chest, the electric guitars had this great lead going on, and off I went, *bustin'* out like a rock star, when very quickly I realized that I was in the wrong key! For those of you who aren't musically inclined, that means I was singing loud and proud, but strong and wrong! Very wrong! The band was playing one tune, and I was singing another. A "wrong-key" intro is an automatic "crash and burn" and it was quite embarrassing to say the least.

I hate to make mistakes. One mistake like that could haunt me for three sleepless nights, tossing and turning, wondering how I could mess up like that on the Sabbath—*leadin'* the *singin'* in the sanctuary? But I've learned and I'm still learning that God does not expect perfection from me. I think sometimes we get "excellence" mixed up with "exactness."

God just wants a heart He can use. All gifts aside, He really just needs someone who will show up. Humbling, isn't it? But what a load off! I have a long list of embarrassing moments, but there's not one moment that God, in His infinite grace, couldn't have used if He needed to with or without my help. So be encouraged!

If you have a willing heart, there's nothing God can't do through you. Sing it loud and sing it proud, and let God do the rest. He will. And by the way, as soon as I get to Heaven, the first thing I'm going to do is audition for the His Band with my new "glorified" voice. I can't wait to lead worship with heavenly hosts as my back-up singers!

"But he said to me, 'My grace is sufficient for you, for my power is made perfect in weakness.' Therefore I will boast all the more gladly about my weaknesses, so that Christ's power may rest on me" (2 Corinthians 12:9 NIV).

*Lord, what a relief to know that I do not have to be perfect or have it all together in order to be used by You! You take my feeble attempts to honor and serve You and turn them into life-changing events…for me and sometimes for those who are in range of the grace splashing around me. Thank You for the talents and gifts You've entrusted to my care. Give me the courage to bust out like a rock star.*

# Lean into the Sun

Lynn Mosher

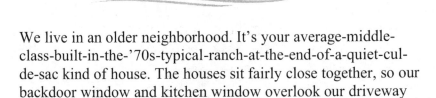

We live in an older neighborhood. It's your average-middle-class-built-in-the-'70s-typical-ranch-at-the-end-of-a-quiet-cul-de-sac kind of house. The houses sit fairly close together, so our backdoor window and kitchen window overlook our driveway and the neighbor's side and back yards.

Standing as a wall of separation along the edge of the driveway is the neighbor's chain-link fence where the previous owner loved to plant things. The fruits of her labor protrude over the fence, concealing the chain-links in a wall of green foliage.

The other morning, as I waited for my second cup of coffee to reheat in the microwave, I looked out the backdoor window to enjoy the view of my side of the garden. The brightness of spring had pounced out from behind winter's shadows and awakened the neighbor's sleeping rosebush with its streams of sunlight beaming down along the fence.

As I stared at this now fifteen foot tall "bush," the profuseness of its cheery rosebuds thrusting themselves into the sunshine looked like little, pink heads with pixy faces, straining to absorb every ounce of warmth and light from the sun that was possible. As the little, rose pixy heads had blossomed on our side of the fence, their beauty was obscured from the neighbor's view. I

146

thought, "Lord, the neighbors aren't enjoying these beauties as much as we are."

Then, the Lord impressed me with the thought that this is a picture of death with its wall of separation. Though obscured from our view, those who have left this earthly life have, in reality, blossomed on life's other side. If Jesus said that those who believe in Him have everlasting life and that He was the vine, then, as Believers in Christ, those of us who continue in our earthly existence remain united with those in heaven.

Though physically separated, we continue to be linked together through the eternal life of the Vine. A smile then spread across my face, as the Lord whispered to my spirit, "The beauty of life on your side of heaven may fade and disappear, but it gains a new quality as they blossom on My side of heaven's fence. Just as the outburst of beauty of My roses comes from leaning into the sun, so, too, the beauty of My children comes from leaning into My Son. Whether on earth or here with Me, beauty explodes in profuseness when they lean into their Source of warmth, peace, love, and joy."

Filled with that peace, love, and joy from my companionship with my Source, I took my coffee, walked into the family room, and leaned into the warmth of the Son.

"I am the Vine, you are the branches. When you're joined with Me and I with you, the relation intimate and organic, the harvest is sure to be abundant" (John 15:5 MSG).

*Father, I thank You that because of Your love for us all, You sent Jesus to be the connecting Vine to eternal life. As we are*

147

*each a part of the Vine as a branch, we are connected to that eternal life, and death has no separation from You. Please help me to stay sensitive to the Holy Spirit, so I may continually lean into the warmth of the sun.*

# A View of Love and Hope

Kathy Cheek

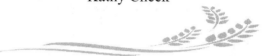

When we moved to Dallas, Texas, six years ago after living in Houston, Texas, for twenty-five years, my husband and I had the opportunity to visit many churches, and we have entered a variety of different sanctuaries all over the city and surrounding area. One of those church visits was a couple weeks before Christmas, and it moved me deeply as I viewed a perfect demonstration of love and hope.

It was the video of an annual Christmas ministry that had just taken place the weekend before. The video began with showing the line—the extremely long, long line of hundreds of people coming down a sidewalk and into this church to go through a "Christmas Store" that had been set up with new donated items of toys, clothes, blankets, and much more for the families in need in their community.

Parents were able to pick out gifts for every member of their family and then could go to specific tables set up to help with wrapping. As they arrived and lined up outside, you could see sadness and hopelessness etched deep on many of the faces. But in the room with the gifts and the volunteers, their hopelessness changed to excitement, hope, and joy. There was a great need, and the need was met above and beyond their expectations.

I honestly don't know who was smiling the most. Was it the families as they received a provision of gifts for their children and loved ones? Was it the volunteers who tirelessly yet lovingly worked to wrap gifts? Everyone was smiling in this room filled with hope! I smiled too and felt like crying at the same time (happy tears) as I watched this beautiful demonstration of love.

My heart experienced a strong tugging as I was reminded to give more generously to people in need each Christmas season. That is something we can all do at Christmas…and throughout the entire year.

"By this all will know that you are My disciples, if you have love for one another" (John 13:35 NKJV).

*Lord, open our hearts to be giving and generous so that others may be blessed this Christmas season. Let this love and hope continue throughout the year as we serve the people of our communities who have need.*

# Being Still

Sara McDaniel

If I'm being real and honest, my life currently is far from simple, and I'm having a hard time "being still." Because I work with schools and districts, August is completely bananas. I'm on and off airplanes and in and out of my car and hotels more times than I care to count this month. I have lots of super early morning meetings and really late evening events that keep me up way past my bedtime. (If you know me well, you know how much I love early to bed, early to rise.)

So this morning, the Lord blessed me by waking me up earlier than usual and graciously giving me some time to be still. Porch sittin' and coffee drinkin' as the sun peaked over the horizon…rare in this season.

It's funny how He works. Sometimes I just cry in awe of His presence when I can feel Him near and when I can feel the stillness. And for me, the best way I can experience this is to wake up early before the craziness of the day takes over. It just does something good for my heart. It soothes my spirit and calms my soul. His mercies are new every morning and to experience the birth of a new day personifies His Great faithfulness!

There are several devotionals I read each morning. One of my favorites comes into my email around 4:00 am and is ready for me as I start my quiet time. Today's *Daily Hope* by Rick Warren just happened to focus "being still" on a morning the Lord woke me early to "be still." Can I get an amen for a divine appointment?

Being still is hard sometimes. I'll be the first to admit it. But the peace that comes in the stillness is priceless. May we all desire the stillness and the harmony it brings to our spirit and soul.

"Be still, and know that I am God; I will be exalted among the nations, I will be exalted in the earth" (Psalm 46:10 NIV).

*God, I want to sit in Your presence and bask in the glow of your glory as the sun tips over the horizon. Even though I am in a busy season of life, I know you can fill me with your peace and calm my spirit with Your faithfulness.*

# Roasting Marshmallows

Vicki Beck

Tonight the men in my husband's small group roasted marshmallows on our back porch. It was hot and muggy outside and I could see sweat dripping down their faces; but their laughter was contagious, drawing my daughter and I outside to join them. The men meet weekly in our home for Christian accountability, sharing their lives and Christ with one another.

Their walk with Christ is stronger because of the relationship they share through Him. But on this night, they were sharing the art of preparing s'mores with one of the guys who had never heard of the infamous campfire treat. They had all the necessary ingredients on hand: a couple bags of marshmallows, a box of graham crackers and several thick Hershey's chocolate candy bars.

I watched as they took turns loading their hanger with marshmallows and then holding the hanger close to the flames from their makeshift "campfire" on our patio. Instructions for roasting the "perfect marshmallow" were exchanged. Chocolate was slipped in place between two graham crackers, ready to receive the puffy, golden brown marshmallows which would melt the chocolate, warm the crackers and transform the ingredients into the rich, delicious dessert known simply as s'mores.

While they laughed and slapped one another on the back enjoying the experience and fellowship, I offered a silent prayer of thanks to God for surrounding my husband with Godly men and for allowing my daughter and me to witness their joy in one another and the Lord. What a beautiful and perfect thing it is when God's people come together in His name and roast marshmallows.

"Two are better than one because they have a good return for their work: If one falls down, his friend can help him up! But pity the man who falls and has no one to help him up....Though one may be overpowered, two can defend themselves. A cord of three strands is not quickly broken" (Ecclesiastes 4:9-12 NIV).

*Thank you, Lord, for marshmallows and the simple joys in life which remind us of Your presence, and for friendships which strengthen and sustain our relationship with You. I pray we remain faithful to You in all we say and do.*

# Books Everywhere

Tammi Slavin

I love to read! I know many people who share my passion. Reading is such a wonderful way to learn new information, provide entertainment, and is one of my absolute favorite things to do. I have read Christian books to help me grow spiritually, motivational books for personal development, medical books to develop professionally, fiction books as an escape, and everything in between!

Some of the books that I have read over the years have left such a strong impression on me that I feel forever connected to the author. However, I will say that if I were on a deserted island and could bring only one book, it would be the Bible. What other answer would one expect from a Christian? I love to read the Bible. When I devote time to reading God's Word, my mood is uplifted and my day invariably goes better.

Although I enjoy my Bible, I admit that I don't read it enough. I devote pitifully too little time to the most important God-inspired book. I know that the Bible is truly a Living Book, and that it has the power to transform me closer to the image of Christ. After all, as a Christ-follower, this is truly the only reading guide I should ever need.

When I think of the thousands of hours spent reading in my life, the reading that truly counted was that done in the Bible. Don't get me wrong; there are some powerfully awesome Christian books out there that illuminate Biblical principals in ways many of us may not see for ourselves. But I can't help but think that God doesn't want me to receive His Word second-hand only.

I need to go straight to the source! I have lately made a commitment to spend considerably more time reading God's Word than reading man's word. To do anything less would be cheating myself out of the richness of a full and intimate relationship with my Savior.

"For the word of God is living and active. Sharper than any double-edged sword, it penetrates even to dividing soul and spirit, joint and marrow; it judges the thoughts and attitudes of the heart" (Hebrews 4:12 NIV).

*Father, thank You for thinking so much of me to give me the Bible. I know that it is truly Your Word, and an instruction manual for my life. Forgive me for not living the full Christian life You want for me; help me to devote the best part of the day to reading Your Word.*

# One Step at at Time

Jeannie De La Garza

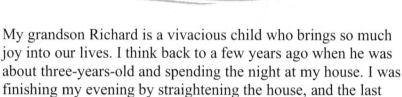

My grandson Richard is a vivacious child who brings so much joy into our lives. I think back to a few years ago when he was about three-years-old and spending the night at my house. I was finishing my evening by straightening the house, and the last thing on my list was to take the trash out. I told Richard he could stand inside the doorway of our den and wait for me while I took out the trash. I explained that I would be right back.

I will never forget the horrified look on his little face. He looked like he was about to cry. I asked him to come with me, but he wouldn't. It had just gotten dark outside, and I had some little stepping stones that led a trail to the trash barrel. I knew I had to get Richard to trust me, so I told him that once I stepped on a stone, I would then tell him when to take his step. We finally started out down the path, and he put his hand into mine.

I told him I would never let anything happen to him. Instantly, his little hand relaxed; and although he was still worried, he wasn't terrified. We took one stone at a time until we got to our destination. I tossed the bag into the trash can, swung Richard into my arms and headed back to the safety of house. I was so humbled by his trust in me. Sometime later, I found out in a conversation with Richard that the reason he was so worried was because he was afraid that a "ninja" was going to get me.

He had been watching his uncle's *Teenage Mutant Ninja Turtles* movie. Richard's trust in me reminds me of how Jesus wants us to trust Him—like little children. Jesus has never failed me. I want to always trust Him in every area of my life. He alone is worthy of my ultimate faith, whether I can see my next step or not. There have been seasons in my life when I couldn't see the next stepping-stone on my path; but as long as I hold Jesus' hand, I know I am safe. The longer I know Him, the more assured I am that I can trust Him every step of the way.

"We live by faith, not by sight" (2 Corinthians 5:7 NIV).

*Father, I thank You that You are always with me. Please always remind me that I can trust You in every season of my life. Right now tell me what I need to hand over to You in complete faith.*

# Praying for Her

Tammy Andrus

I sat in the pew with my eyes closed and head bowed while the pastor was praying one Sunday morning. As I meditated on God, He revealed a face in my mind of an old friend I hadn't seen in years. He laid it upon my heart to pray for her. I prayed for her then, but for the next several weeks, God continually impressed on me to offer my old friend up in prayer.

I prayed for her daily, though I didn't understand what I was specifically praying for. I had lost contact with her, so I had no way of reaching her. Finally, while driving in the car, God again urged me to pray for my friend. I did, but this time I asked God to please reveal to me why I had been praying diligently for my friend these past several weeks. I needed affirmation for the spiritual step of prayer I was taking in my walk with Christ.

I arrived at the store to which I was driving and parked in the parking lot. I glanced out the window before getting out of the car and guess who was sitting in the car in front of me? It was my old friend I had been praying for. I immediately got out of my car and went to her. She was upset and obviously had been crying. She talked with me for several minutes and told me that she had been going through some rough times and that she was confronted with many difficult decisions.

I told her that several weeks ago God laid it on my heart to pray for her. God used me to show her that He cared about her struggles and that He loved her, and she was comforted. I know my friend saw God that day, and I'm glad that I was obedient to God and prayed for my friend without understanding why.

"Therefore confess your sins to each other and pray for each other so that you may be healed. The prayer of a righteous man is powerful and effective" (James 5:16 NIV).

*Lord, please encourage me to pray diligently for those you have laid upon my heart. Help me to take only a few moments out of my busy day to pray because I know that my prayer will be both powerful and effective.*

# Lessons from Loss

Stacey Tuley

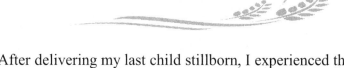

After delivering my last child stillborn, I experienced the most excruciating pain in my heart. It is just not natural to labor, deliver, and not bring your child home with you. Nothing made sense about the entire situation, but I did find God's comfort in the midst of my deep pain in knowing He was with me even when I didn't feel His presence all of the time. That's where my faith kicked in.

I felt so much love and support from my church family, but there was an emptiness that I couldn't explain or fill. I went to work as a nurse after my two other kids started school because I didn't want to sit a home and cry about being alone. I wasn't going to let this destroy me, so I thought I'd help others who were grieving. It seemed that hurting people were the only ones that I could relate to.

Eventually, I ended up back at home alone after suffering a back and neck injury from lifting patients with my already frail back. However, I was finally able to face the silence and the loneliness. I heard an evangelist who lost his wife in an automobile accident say that he didn't start dealing with his grief until he quit asking God "Why?" and started asking Him "What now?"

When I began to take my focus off of why Anna had to die and put it on what I needed to do now, God could work in my life. Our human minds often cannot comprehend and deal with the why. Asking why only led me further down the path of depression and blame. When I began to ask God what I needed to do now, I began to focus on the here and now. The biggest what and now was my family. They were there all along needing me.

I had to give myself permission to shed a tear from time to time, but not to stay in the grief. When the tears slowed, I would thank God for keeping Anna safe in His arms and for keeping me alive to raise my other two children and to be a support to my husband. As I began to thank God for all of the blessings in my life, and really look hard for them, God lifted my spirit and comforted me. I find so much joy in the little things. I especially cherish and love the time I have with my family and friends.

"Blessed are those who mourn, for they shall be comforted" (Matthew 5:4 NIV).

*Dear God, I thank You for Your promises and that You show no favoritism to Your children. What You do for one, You will do for another. I thank You that as You have shown me comfort, You will comfort my brothers and sisters in Christ. Let them know that You are with them and that they will laugh again. Fill them with Your peace and joy again. Refresh their hearts and minds and fill them with strength and courage to face each new day.*

# A Few Minutes Alone

Sunny Reed

I just want a few minutes alone! I get up half an hour early to read my Bible and pray and here she is at my side, putting her feet all over me while I try and start my day with God. How am I supposed to have a meaningful conversation with the Creator while my three-year-old is staring at me with her feet on top of my Bible?

I mention my frustration to my dad one early morning while we drank coffee. When I visit back home, I always get up extra early to be alone with my father before he goes to work.

"Oh yes, I remember those days," he says as he puts down his Bible. "Except you started that when you were two. As soon as you heard me stirring the coffee, you were by my side." My father smiles at the memory.

"Oh," I say slightly dumbfounded because what I am complaining about is what I'm doing to my dad at the exact moment, except now I am twenty-eight-years old! Funny thing is I always had an inherent feeling that every day began with Bible and coffee. Maybe my daughter feels the same way because she has learned it from watching me.

I realize that there is clearly a lesson to be learned here. I am determined that from now on I will try and treasure those early morning times with my daughter, expressing to her the same love and patience I had been given and was still being given by my father. My prayer is that my daughter will not know how to drink coffee in the morning without her Bible, and that she too will have an inherent feeling that she cannot start her day without first spending time with God.

"Fix these words of mine to your hearts and minds; tie them as symbols on your hands and bind them on your foreheads. Teach them to your children, talking about them when you sit at home and when you walk along the road, when you lie down and when you get up" (Deuteronomy 11:18-19 NIV).

*Lord, help me to see the big picture in the middle of my daily tasks. Help me guide my children with Your words and teach Your words to them diligently.*

# The Search

Kerry Johnson

---

I was laying on the floor of our boys' bedroom one afternoon, peering behind their bunk beds, when Cole walked in. "Help me look for Spike," I mumbled. "I can't find him."

The Johnson house is a critter haven, one of which is a bright green, sixteen-inch long Chinese Water Dragon named Spike. Spike is allowed loose in our boys' lizard-proof bedroom for a couple of hours each day, and he often hides out on the tall fake tree next to the window. Occasionally, he scrambles off the tree and hides when he's frightened.

I figured that's what happened this particular time, but as Cole and I searched their room, our concern increased. We checked behind and under the bookshelves and the dresser and even in the closet, though it had been closed.

When Chase poked his blond head through the doorway, he noted our desperate search. "Are you looking for Spike?" Chase asked, a big grin lifting his cheeks. "Did you check his cage?" He jabbed a thumb toward Spike's large terrarium, where our beloved pet lizard was indeed basking on the branches below his UV light. "I put him away." Chase giggled at the surprised look on my face, and Cole and I let out twin sighs of relief and chagrin.

Later, I thought of the many places we search for God's will in our lives. We read books and devotionals, ask friends, family, and pastors, pray for guidance, even mimic others' faith journeys in an effort to find God's will. These are not necessarily bad or wrong, but often the obvious source for spiritual guidance and heavenly help gets overlooked—the Word.

After all, God's Word is a proven "lamp to our feet and a light to our path" (Psalm 119:105 NKJV). Start the search for God's best for you in the Word, because the Author created His Book specifically as a living, eternal map to lead us through any situation in life.

"You are my hiding place and my shield; I hope in Your word" (Psalm 119:114 NKJV).

*Heavenly Father, thank You for giving us the Bible to guide our days. Help us keep Your Living Word open and read and warm in our hands. Help us to read the Bible to our families, hide it in our hearts, and live in its pages, keeping our eyes on Jesus.*

# Parental Substitute

### Tasha Schaded

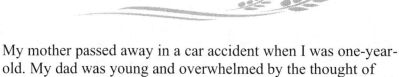

My mother passed away in a car accident when I was one-year-old. My dad was young and overwhelmed by the thought of raising three children, so he gave us to his parents to raise. I can remember thinking when I was a child that my life was normal. Everyone had to know what it was like not to know your mother.

As I started getting older, I realized that it wasn't normal. All my friends had mothers and fathers and all lived together like one happy family. About 3rd grade, I can remember crying on Mother's Day because I didn't have a mom. My grandparents would try to comfort me by telling me God needed her and she was an angel in heaven watching over me.

I didn't understand why my mother was taken, and her death made me mad at God. Now that I am a mother, I look back on my life and thank God that He gave me my wonderful grandparents. I think to myself, "What kind of person would I be if my parents would have raised me?"

I think that I am a better person because of my grandparents. I had security, consistency, and so much love. I now try to raise my children with the morals and values that my grandparents raised me with. I know now that God put these awesome people in my life for a reason. I am a stronger, more compassionate person because of them.

My dad passed away about three years ago, and I know my parents are together in heaven. One day I'll be with them both. I know they will be pleased with how my grandparents raised me, and they will be proud of the woman I have become.

"A father to the fatherless, a defender of widows, is God in his holy dwelling. God sets the lonely in families, he leads out the prisoners with singing; but the rebellious live in a sun-scorched land" (Psalm 68:5-6 NIV).

*Dear Lord, I thank You so much for the wonderful people You have placed in my life. I don't always look at my situation as Your will, Lord. Please help me to see the blessings around me, even in the storms in my life. I thank You for the people You have blessed me with.*

# Tough Times Encouragement

Ann Cornelius

When the stock market took a plunge recently, it reminded me to put my trust in the God who loves me. Looking back over my life, I can remember the times that God has carried me in ways that defy all reason.

In 1973, my children were 5-years-old and 6-months-old. After a trying situation at the hospital, I quit my job. Two weeks later, my husband was laid off from his job. I really prayed for wisdom and another job.

After my two-week notice was complete, my supervisor tried to get me to take back my resignation. But I felt strongly that I should look for another job. The following week I started looking for a job, and out of the blue, the NASA Dispensary Supervisor called me for a temporary job on Skylab.

I had applied for a job at the NASA Dispensary two years before, and they just happened to reopen my application. The supervisor asked me to come in for an interview the next morning. After the interview, I was hired to start immediately with a very nice salary increase. The job lasted for 11 months and was the beginning of my new career as an occupational health nurse.

After the experience of working at the NASA Dispensary, I was able to work in the Houston area in occupational health for several different companies for over 34 years. I have learned to trust God during times of crisis because He has proven Himself faithful in every circumstance.

"Don't worry about anything; instead, pray about everything. Tell God what you need, and thank him for all he has done" (Philippians 4:6 NLT).

*Father, help me to rely on You when times get tough. I want to not worry but walk in obedience in accordance to the plan that You have for me. Help me to trust You during the good times and the bad.*

# A Plank in My Eye

Joan Hall

While driving to work one day, I came upon a line of slow moving cars. There wasn't any reason for traffic to move slowly except the lead car was traveling a maximum of forty-five miles per hour.

"I don't believe this," I said to myself. "This person has three cars delayed because they refuse to drive the speed limit." I couldn't wait to find a passing zone on the rural farm-to-market road. Looking in the rear view mirror, I saw another fast moving car approach. "Make it four cars," I said, as the car behind me accelerated and passed all four automobiles.

"What is he doing? That's crazy! He's in a no passing zone and near a hill. I hope he reaches his destination without killing himself or someone else." Less than two minutes later, I took the opportunity to pass; however, I was also in a no passing zone and near an even taller hill.

I was so quick to judge the other driver, and then I did something worse. It made me realize that I often tend to judge other Christians. I look upon their sin as being worse than my own. After all, I've not committed murder. At times, I have been angry with other Christians. I've never been guilty of armed robbery, but what about the paper clip I "borrowed" and never returned from my employer.

Jesus tells us only when we first take the plank out of our own eye will we be able to see the speck in our brother's eye. However, I've come to realize there will always be planks in my eye. All Christians will sin, but praise God through His grace we are always forgiven. Since that morning, I've seen that same slow moving automobile several times, but I'm reminded to always remove the plank from my eye.

"Why do you look at the speck of sawdust in your brother's eye and pay no attention to the plank in your own eye? How can you say to your brother, 'Let me take the speck out of your eye,' when all the time there is a plank in your own eye?" (Matthew 7:3-4 NIV).

*Heavenly Father, thank You for Your saving grace. Forgive me for the times when I judge another brother or sister. Help me to remember to remove the plank in my eye.*

# Simply Me

Maryleigh Bucher

I learned that long ago some doors—friendships, opportunities, employments—would close because *Simply Me* wasn't good enough. Yet, other doors opened because I was courageous enough to be *Simply Me*. I had to decide which doors were meant to close and which doors I needed to boldly walk through. *Simply Me* would not have been welcome in every door, and I didn't want to change who I was in order to squeeze my way in.

*Simply Me* could have been someone else—someone I was not created to be. After all, God made me to be *Simply Me*, and I finally discovered who I am. I am an organizer with side-ways humor and ideas and thoughts bursting inside to come out. I am a status-quo reformer with a bold voice that offers awkwardly hugging words. I gather information, asking questions because I know someone out there is also curious. Maybe she's like I used to be—afraid to use my voice. Afraid to be *Simply Me*.

I learned that I could go out each day and be who God created me to be. To do otherwise would be to reject His design for my life. Yes, there is an entire outside world with people who have the power to open and close doors. But I can't be who my mom wants me to be, my husband wants me to be, my sons want me to be, or even my friends want me to be. I need to be who God created me to be—*Simply Me*.

Are you scared to show the outside world that God created you to be *Simply You?* Learn from me and don't change to fit into doors that are not meant for you. God will open the right ones where *Simple Me* belongs. We must all untangle ourselves from the perceptions that don't line up with His design. We can accept the *Simply You* in others and let them see the *Simply Me* in us. We are all liberated as God's Children to be who He created us to be and love others and ourselves as we are: *Simply Me and Simply You.*

"Your eyes saw my unformed body; all the days ordained for me were written in your book before one of them came to be. How precious to me are your thoughts, God! How vast is the sum of them!" (Psalm 139:16-17 NIV).

*Father, help me to see what You see in me. Open my eyes to how all these different parts of me fit together—to see the intrinsic beauty of Your design. You aren't surprised by the Simple Me and the Simply You in all of us. Show me the open doors that You have prepared for me and let me never change to fit into doors that aren't for me.*

# Not Supposed to be Here

Estella Smith

After leaving the family nest to go to college, I got a little off track. I strayed from the path. I wasn't going crazy, like going out partying and drinking. I just was lost because I did not have a good Christian foundation. I was five hours from home without a church and church-going friends.

Every day was the same: I went to class and hung out with friends. I was living in my own world that I had fooled myself into believing was good. Then, one day I believe God got tired of watching me wander around aimlessly, so He called out to me.

He woke me up and told me to look around and see the chaos. I had created this chaos by living a life that I thought was great. Boy! Did I get a wake-up call. I look back now and see that I was in a trance. My life seemed perfect, but it was an illusion the enemy had created.

When God spoke, it was like a veil lifted from my eyes, allowing me to see the real world I was living in. When I looked around me and saw the truth, I thought I would die! I, of course, asked God the classic questions: *How could I have gotten here? How could I have allowed myself to get so lost? I was completely blind!*

175

Now when I look back, I can start to gain understanding of why my life unfolded as it did. I also know why God allowed me to get to that low point in my life. He showed me that when I forgot about Him, He never forgot about me. He was always there for me and always will be. Now I never lose sight of Him.

There is no worse feeling than waking from a bad dream and realizing that you're living it. I did not realize how lost I was until my Father reached out His hand and walked me back home.

"Suppose one of you has a hundred sheep and loses one of them. Does he not leave the ninety-nine in the open country and go after the lost sheep until he finds it? And when he finds it, he joyfully puts it on his shoulders and goes home. Then he calls his friends and neighbors together and says, 'Rejoice with me; I have found my lost sheep'" (Luke 15:4-6 NIV).

*Lord, there are times when I find myself where I'm not supposed to be, and somehow You are always there to guide me back. Thank You for remembering me even when I forget You. I pray for those in my life who are lost and need to be brought back home.*

# God's Provisions

Cynthia Faulkner

Returning home from a mission trip to Ecuador, God laid this message upon my heart. Think of a time when you have struggled financially in your life. Perhaps you were not sure how to pay all your bills, or you had to scrape together loose change to buy a loaf of bread. Remember what it took to make it through that tough time. Perhaps you borrowed money, sold or pawned a possession, or applied for public assistance.

Now, think of what you felt—frustration, despair, fear, hopelessness, or shame. Missionaries in Ecuador and other poor countries minister to people who also have struggles. Some Ecuadorians wake up wondering how they will feed their family and whether they will be able to earn or beg money that day.

If their child gets sick, how will they pay medical expenses? They do not have possessions to sell for such emergencies. They experience their struggles every day, not as just a period in their life; yet, they do not despair, fear or feel shame or hopelessness.

You see, they have learned to depend on God for all their needs. They find Him sufficient, even in their daily struggles. Our mission group provided thirteen villages with food provisions. Each church family received enough food to last a family of four in the U.S. about one week, but it will last them six months and will feed a family two or three times the size.

At a church in Zabala, two baskets were set on each side of the altar where inside were placed small amounts of the food the church members had received. The church families in Ecuador do not have money for tithes; instead, they tithe a tenth of their precious provisions trusting that God will bless them with even more.

"God blesses the people who patiently endure testing. Afterwards they will receive the crown of life that God has promised to those who love him" (James 1:12 NIV).

*Dear Heavenly Father, help me to remember that regardless of the difficulties I am going through, that I am in Your care. Remind me that You are sufficient, and I lay at your feet.*

# A Freely Given Gift

Bernadine Zimmerman

It was a beautiful summer afternoon. My husband and I had decided to take a relaxing walk in the park. As was his routine, he took some bread to feed the ducks. When we first arrived, there were no ducks on the side of the pond where we were standing. My husband didn't let that disappoint him. He started feeding a lone muskrat that was lazily swimming by. I quickly grew bored, sat on a bench, and focused on something on my phone. A few minutes later, I heard an excited, "Honey, check this out!"

At the sound of my husband's excited voice, I looked up from my phone. I stared in amazement at the sight that greeted my eyes. Swimming across the pond, as if they were late for an appointment, was a large group of ducks, drawn as if by a magnet to the bread he was tossing into the water. I was shocked because just moments before they were all on the other side of the pond and were showing no interest in moving.

The scene of the ducks swimming enthusiastically across the pond was compelling. The bread was tossed into the water for whomever desired it. The ducks swam a good distance in hopes that they would get a few pieces of the freely given bread. I noticed, however, that not all the ducks came.

Maybe they had already eaten. Perhaps they were tired, and the distance felt too far. Maybe it seemed too good to be true. Whatever the reason, they chose not to come. I thought about the action of some of the ducks that didn't accept my husband's freely given gift. It reminded me of the gift of salvation.

This gift is offered freely to everyone. Unfortunately, not everyone desires or accepts the gift. The job of every Christian is to offer the gift and to rejoice with those who accept it. Those who don't accept—maybe they will another day. But until then, we'll keep feeding, praying, hoping and believing that all will accept the freely given gift of salvation.

"The Spirit and the bride say, 'Come!' And let the one who hears say, 'Come!' Let the one who is thirsty come; and let the one who wishes take the free gift of the water of life" (Revelation 22:17 NIV).

*Father, I understand that not everyone will accept Jesus as their Lord and Savior right away. However, that will not stop me from spreading seeds of salvation to those around me. I pray that those seeds will eventually take root, get watered and sprout tender shoots of faith.*

# Calm in the Storm

Susie Mozisek

I have often heard people say about those going through a difficult time, "You should see how strong they were. Not one tear was shed as the news was given. What faith they must have." I am not one of those people. When I get bad news or am experiencing a difficult time, you will hear me and see me show my heartache.

Recently, as my husband was undergoing emergency surgery for an infection following his hip replacement, I found myself in an out of control situation. I cried out to God. I shed many tears. I even emotionally lost it while talking to a friend on the phone. I was all alone, four hours from my home, and saying goodbye to my husband outside the operating room. We were both scared of the risks and unsure of the procedure that had to be done.

As I went out to sit in an empty waiting room at 9:00 pm, I noticed a small chapel down the hallway. I went to the altar and threw myself on my knees and cried out to God to please heal my husband and make this fear I was feeling go away. After praying aloud for a while with my hands lifted to the sky, I opened my eyes and saw an open Bible lying in front of me.

My instinctive reaction was to turn to the familiar verses of comfort I had known for years. Instead, I was drawn to a page

181

marked in Psalms. I started to read Psalm 141:1-2 and the tears started streaming. God had a special verse just for me: "O Lord, I am calling to you. Please hurry! Listen when I cry to you for help! Accept my prayer as incense offered to you, and my upraised hands as an evening offering."

God not only knew my circumstances, He showed me that He knew what time of day it was, and He was listening. At that moment, a sudden peace came over me and I knew things would be okay. Shortly after, some family members arrived, as well as the surgeon with good news. The infection had most likely not reached the hip joint. We praised God and asked Him for further healing.

Even if the outcome would have been different, we know God was there every step of the way. I wish I could say that God always speaks so clearly to me. When He does, it is the most amazing thing to experience. When He doesn't, I try to hold to His truths that have held true for centuries past and continue to hold true today.

"For the word of God is living and active. Sharper than any double-edged sword, it penetrates even to dividing soul and spirit, joints and marrow; it judges the thoughts and attitudes of the heart. Nothing in all creation is hidden from God's sight. Everything is uncovered and laid bare before the eyes of him to whom we must give an account" (Hebrews 4:12-13 NIV).

*Lord, I thank You for Your precious Word that can comfort, guide and even assure me in times of uncertainty. Let me always turn to You first through the good times as well as the bad.*

# God Winks

Dixie Phillips

Grandma Eleanor was the stabilizing force in my life for as long as I can remember. Her wisdom and common sense echoed in the depths of my soul. After her death, it seemed the grief would come in waves and cast shades of suffocating bereavement throughout my day. I would always find comfort in the Scriptures and consolation in the old hymns about Heaven.

But as our family was embarking on a new adventure, I was stung by this painful reality—Grandma Eleanor wouldn't be part of my daughter's wedding. As my daughter, Rebekah, and I made wedding preparations, I discovered a treasured picture of Grandma Eleanor cradling our newborn, Beka, in her arms. Hot tears slipped down my cheeks. I wish Grandma could be here. She would know exactly how many pounds of strawberries and bananas we needed for the chocolate fountain.

She could also help Rebekah and me with the theme for the wedding. We decided since Rebekah was marrying Zacharia David Fox, that "The Fox Tale Begins" would fit the bill. We hunted for tiny, imitation foxtails in hopes of making cute wedding favors with our witty slogan, but we weren't having any luck. As I looked at the picture of my beloved grandmother, a small box caught my eye.

When Grandma Eleanor died, my father had given me the box which held a few of her knick-knacks. I opened the plain cardboard box and saw a tiny package with a stained Martha Washington one and one-half-cent stamp fastened in the corner and a faded label addressed to Mrs. Eleanor Holtz. I lifted the lid off and gasped when I saw a tiny foxtail attached to a white leather bookmark that was etched with a gold imprint of a fox.

It was a "God wink" for me, and it brought such comfort to my grieving soul. As my fingers traced the soft foxtail, I pondered the delightful, heavenly gift. Could it be that Grandma Eleanor was a member of that great cloud of witnesses? Could she be cheering us on? Is it possible she already knew that her great-granddaughter will soon be married?

I may never know this side of Heaven the answers to my questions, but this one thing I know—the Holy Spirit takes great pleasure in comforting grieving hearts. So, let the Fox Tale begin!

"Therefore, since we are surrounded by such a great cloud of witnesses, let us throw off everything that hinders and the sin that so easily entangles, and let us run with perseverance the race marked out for us" (Hebrews 12:1 NIV).

*Lord, thank You for the God Winks that You give Your faithful servants throughout the day. You take time to let each of Your children know that You care about them. Help me to be in tuned to the Holy Spirit, so I can see all the special blessings You give to me.*

# Spirit and Truth

Susan Wood

I've been marveling about the "special place" that I enter into with the Lord in prayer. This place is like our personal zone that contains only Him and me. It's a meeting space that exists just for me and the Lord—our own special, private place.

This week I saw this special place as kind of a cone. I was thinking about our relationship within this cone. I have heard that some people try to connect with the Lord by doing a behavior, like speaking in tongues for a certain amount of time, reading the New Testament over and over, or spending a set number of minutes or hours with the Lord.

I thought of how I would feel if my grown children came to spend quality time with me and just said certain things each time or clocked how much time they were spending with me. I would not like it, nor would that make me feel loved and valued. I would desire for them to relax with me and be totally themselves—completely open, honest, true and sincere.

In my special cone, I connect and communicate with Him through the Spirit of God, and it's the Holy Spirit that bonds us together. It's a place of revealing real truth—instead of trying to hide things, make excuses or blame others. I must admit everything in complete truth and take full responsibility, acknowledging any sin or weakness on my part. Being in full truth is being completely transparent, willing to confess my sins, shortcomings, inabilities and weaknesses to the Lord. It's admitting I'm not what I desire to be, and I fall short and am needy.

It's also a place to acknowledge my strengths and realize they come from Him. I am blessed and strong in many areas, and I have God to thank for it. This cone is a special place to draw from the well of thankfulness that's deep in my heart for everything He has given me. I truly appreciate all the blessings that I have, and this cone of Spirit and Truth is a meeting place to talk and reflect on God's abundance, and drink it in and savor His blessings.

Some days are busy, so I don't get into my special place with the Lord. But I can't go long without meeting with Him. If it's been a while since I've entered our cone, I feel like I'm becoming unglued or fading inside. God gives me all the strength I need for life, and I can't last long without Him. I absolutely need my relationship with the Lord. He is my lifeline.

"For God is Spirit, so those who worship him must worship in spirit and in truth" (John 4:24 NLT).

*Father, I have found my special place, the cone of Spirit and Truth, with You. I am honored that You would spend time with me, enjoying my presence just as much as I enjoy Yours. Help me to daily enter into our special place, so I can admit my wrongs and fill up on Your goodness.*

# Five Minute Pity Party

Tiffany Locke

People just love pity parties. They are so fun and jam-packed with complaining, whining, and lots of comparing. However, we have to be in a special mood to partake in such a party. I try to make my appearance rare to these parties, but occasionally I find myself being pulled into them. I at least try to limit my stay for only five minutes. Granted there are times when I want to stay longer, but I try really hard to stick with the five-minute rule.

What do these parties have that are so intriguing? They are full of "I want," "I don't have," "Why?" and "That is so not fair!" I have to admit there have been times when throwing a themed "comparing and coveting" pity party in my honor has taken up a lot of my energy. I've had to ask myself, "Is the thrill of the party really worth it?"

I have a choice: I can stay at this party all night and wallow in self-despair or I can go to a different kind of party. The theme of this other party is one of love, confidence and contentment. And the one who set up this party is the best party-thrower of all: God! I am invited to enjoy His party every day. His party is full of forgiveness, blessings, and mercy.

Now, that is a party that I want to attend and stay as long as I can! I know that at God's party I will find joy and peace. My

187

pity parties only leave me feeling hopeless and dissatisfied. God has shown me that my life truly is blessed! I love my kids and my husband. I love the plans that God has for me. I shouldn't covet one particular blessing of another woman. If I do, I might as well ask God for her entire life, and I really don't want that.

Therefore, I choose to leave my self-created pity parties and attend a party where God has presents just for me and music played in my honor. Nevertheless, if I have to throw a pity party, I only stay for five minutes. Then, I hop on over to God's cool party where everyone has fun.

"Be strong and courageous. Do not be afraid or terrified because of them, for the Lord your God goes with you; he will never leave you nor forsake you" (Deuteronomy 31:6 NIV).

*God, I know that there are times when I compare myself to others, and I have a disgruntled attitude. Please forgive me when I throw myself pity parties. Please remind me that I am wonderfully made, and help me to remember that You have a party full of blessings just for me. Please bring to my mind the many presents that You have written my name on.*

# A Sister in Worship

Sunny Reed

This past weekend was our annual women's conference. I had invited friends, neighbors, my mom and sisters. While walking the dog the first morning, I prayed for God to free me and my sisters and our mom of any ailment that might threaten to keep us from receiving what God had in store of us at the conference. I prayed that I would be more concerned about "being" than about hosting while my family was here.

My sister and I barely got out of the house for the first night of the conference on time to meet my friends for dinner at a local bistro. We had to leave my husband with instructions for my three kiddos and my sister's two-year-old. Then we kissed everyone at least three times and changed jewelry and purses twice.

My sister was unbelievably calm driving out of the driveway leaving her only child in the hands of my husband who at the moment wasn't even in the house with the kids! He was content to stand and water plants for who knows how long. When we got to the conference, we were late. Since I had brought seven ladies with me, we couldn't exactly sneak in the front. There were over 2,000 ladies there!

We had to sit way in the back. I was content to watch the crowd and pray for God's movement among such a gathering. As the evening closed, the band played Chris Tomlin's song, "Our GOD," and I happened to look past my friend next to me and over at my sister. It was the most beautiful sight.

My sister, the middle child, meek, sweet, gentle and reserved was standing with both hands straight up in the air, earnestly singing, "Our God is Greater, Our God is Higher…." She was drinking it in. She was unashamed to claim her faith. She was strengthened by the magnitude of faith in this place; she was encouraged by the presence of thousands of women proclaiming their faith.

I am not a crier, but I could not hold back the tears. God had answered my prayers on the first night. He had sweetly chosen to reveal Himself to me through my sister's act of worship.

"Great is the Lord and most worthy of praise; his greatness no one can fathom" (Psalm 145:3 NIV).

*Dear God, thank You for the gift of worship. Thank You for allowing me to experience You through the worship of another. God, You are great and we can never fathom all of You. I praise You for sharing pieces of Your greatness with Your people.*

# His Delight

## Kimberly Dawn Rempel

Hunched over a plastic bowl, she carefully eyes mini-chocolate chips as she eats. Finally, she has it all to herself; big brother has finished his portion. He soon joins her at the coffee table to read a story, possibly to her. He tweets and twitters, unaware of sister's rising suspicion.

She presses her soft arms against the little orange bowl, inching her face ever closer to precious chocolate bits. She watches him from the corner of her eye. Suddenly, she collects a fist full of chocolate chips, jams them in her mouth, then grabs the bowl and runs across the room.

The bowl firmly planted on an empty chair, she glances back at her unperturbed brother, resumes hunching, and eats. From the kitchen I watch, filled with adoration as she greedily hovers over her precious treat. It feels as though my heart may burst from the affection that fills it.

Then I realize that God delights in me that way. I don't judge my daughter for being selfish or greedy—not because it's acceptable behavior, but because I understand that she doesn't know better. When I sin or make a mistake, God isn't scowling with folded arms, ready to give me what I deserve. He remembers that I don't know better and delights in me anyway.

He doesn't condone my actions, but He gives me grace. Thank You, my perfect, loving Father!

"The LORD your God is with you, he is mighty to save. He will take great delight in you, he will quiet you with his love, he will rejoice over you with singing" (Zephaniah 3:17 NIV).

*Thank You, Lord, for Your grace. Thank You that You delight in me and rejoice over me with singing! What an amazing picture of You as my loving Father! Lord, I pray I receive Your grace and it would overflow into the lives of others. I want to extend Your grace to them as freely as I've received it.*

# A Journey to Hope

Susan Shipe

These things don't happen to regular people, or so I thought until our phone rang one early July morning in 2002. The morning was already thick with humidity making even the upholstered chair feel damp. The windows were open wide, and the Appalachian dew clung to the screens—these were the things I noted as I walked to the telephone to end its relentless ringing.

The cry I heard will forever sound in my ear. My grown up girl sobbed at the end of that phone, 700 miles away. The shock was palpable. The distance was like an eternity away—actually a reality away. Yet, it was true and real, and action needed to be taken.

I have one sibling, a sister, I quickly dialed her number. "Peg, her fiancé was murdered last night—I have to go to her."

And so began months and months of sadness, grief, and hopelessness. Fifteen years later, and I remember that morning as though it happened yesterday. It was the time in my life when God showed up and showed off.

The paralyzing grief and despair racked within me. Worship services, the joyous kind with hands clapping and feet tapping, were times of questioning and doubt. My heart continued to break for my daughter, and God was getting an earful from me. Day in and day out.

Several months later on a cold weekday morning—one with ice crystals on the windows—God came. He came to me in the wee hours of darkness of a regular day and began teaching me the biblical principle of hope: "Now may the God of hope fill you with all joy and peace in believing, that you may abound in hope by the power of the Holy Spirit" (Romans 15.13 ESV).

It was this scripture God used to begin my healing. I was in treatment! Hope began to radiate in me, through me, and around me. Today, I celebrate 16 years in remission from hopelessness. I wake up each morning knowing the God of Hope will fill me with joy and peace and will cause me to overflow with His Hope. Joy is a choice—one we must choose each and every day: "Today, I will walk in Joy." Hope is the gift God gives us when we make that conscious choice to embrace it.

"This hope is a strong and trustworthy anchor for our souls. It leads us through the curtain into God's inner sanctuary" (Hebrews 6:19 NLT).

*Father God, in Jesus' Name, every day is in Your hands. You know our going out and coming in. You know the beginning from the end and all the in-between's. Guide us today and surround us with Your love and care.*

# Blessed Toilet Brush

### Christina Ketchum

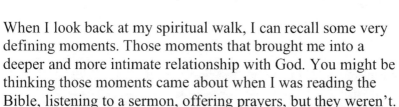

When I look back at my spiritual walk, I can recall some very defining moments. Those moments that brought me into a deeper and more intimate relationship with God. You might be thinking those moments came about when I was reading the Bible, listening to a sermon, offering prayers, but they weren't. It wasn't until recently, in hindsight, that I even acknowledged the importance of these moments.

I describe these defining moments as, "Joyfully Sacrificing My Flesh (Selfishness) for this Insignificant Task with little Appreciation." I'm sorry about the long definition but it has truly changed my life. The concept came about when God forced me beyond my comfort, beyond my pleasure, beyond my physical abilities, beyond my emotional capabilities with tasks that were seemingly insignificant—and for which I got absolutely no acknowledgement.

I have had several of these defining moments, but the one that sticks out to me the most is the one with "My Blessed Toilet Bowl Brush." For several years, I was a stay-at-home mom with three preschool-aged children. At this time, my life revolved around poopy diapers, crying babies, cooking, cleaning and constant isolation.

195

One day, on the verge of a total nervous breakdown, I was using my sliver of precious free time to clean the bathrooms. I grabbed the toilet bowl brush in tears and started cleaning, but after a minute I finally gave up the pity party. I asked God for help then proceeded to "joyfully sacrifice my flesh for this insignificant task with little appreciation" and cleaned my toilets with a smile and a new song in my heart. I basically told God that if this was His will for me, even for the rest of my life, I will choose to be joyful.

There have been hundreds of those defining moments since my blessed toilet bowl brush task and there will be thousands more. Now it wasn't a clean toilet that brought me closer to God. It was a joyful act of obedience in an area that doesn't seem to amount to much with no one around to witness it.

It can be easy to obey when we are feeding the homeless, speaking in front of a large group or leading worship. The world tells us those acts are good and we receive many accolades for them. But God is more interested in the private acts of obedience that we do. This really shows where our hearts are and if our flesh is chipped away enough to handle more of His purpose for us.

Fortunately, I now have two beautiful young ladies who clean my toilets each week. I'm definitely not perfect, but it seems that God believes I've chipped down my flesh enough to bless me with the opportunity to work as a psychotherapist. And I want more! I want more of Him and His will in my life. So anytime my flesh starts screaming and there isn't a single person around to see me throw a pity party, I remind myself that this could be another toilet bowl brush moment. Who knows what

God can make out of this seemingly insignificant (yet extremely difficult) act of obedience!

"Whoever can be trusted with very little can also be trusted with much, and whoever is dishonest with very little will also be dishonest with much" (Luke 16:10 NIV).

*God, You see my small efforts of obedience. Show me how to find peace even in the most insignificant and trivial areas of my life. I want to always pour You into the center of my daily thoughts, words and actions.*

# Blood-Sukers

## Alisa Hope Wagner

Mosquitoes in the car, while you're driving down the highway, are dangerous. These pesky insects are blood-sucking attackers, and an accurate metaphor for spiritual attack. Two weeks of Texas rain has left us with an army of mosquitoes recklessly attacking any warm-blooded animal within buzz reach. They are huge and thirsty.

I got my three kids in the car and started the 20 minute drive to their school. Shouts of "I see one!" and "It's on me!" echoed in my ear. Two times I looked down to swat one away, allowing my car to drift too close to the curb.

*This must stop!* I thought.

"Hold on guys," I said and rolled down all four windows of my SUV.

"What are you doing, Mom?" my first born asked. "You'll let more in!"

"Just watch," I said. "The wind will push them out."

A minute later I rolled back up the windows and the mosquitoes were gone.

So many times we are moving in God's will and there are attacking mosquitoes all around us. We can't just stop what we are doing and focus on them because we are responsible for others. There are people in our vehicle.

Instead of focusing on the attacks, however, if we would simply roll down everything—make ourselves completely vulnerable to God, the Wind of His Presence will rush in and fight for us.

It may seem contradictory to make yourself vulnerable when blood-sucking haters are all around you; but in fact, it allows God the freedom to deal with them. Don't shelter up. Don't shut down. When you are attacked, open up and let the Holy Spirit rush in. He will fight for you. He will redeem you. He will drive those mosquitoes out of your destiny.

Let God in. Trust Him. Keep driving and enjoy the ride.

"For the LORD your God is the one who goes with you to fight for you against your enemies to give you victory" (Deuteronomy 20:4 NIV).

*Lord, when I am attacked by physical and spiritual forces, help me to open the windows of my life, so Your Spirit can pour in. I know that I am not strong enough. Only you can defeat the powers that come against me.*

**August 2018:**

If we had to choose one word to describe our first month in Mombasa, Kenya, it would be *defeated*. Every circumstance around us both in the U.S. and Kenya demanded us to go home! Our daughters and family in U.S were very sick, renters were refusing to pay rent, changes were occurring in our African ministry and the list goes on and on. We were feeling worn down and defeated.

It had been a struggle to not jump on the next plane and take care of all these heavy burdens. The only thing that was getting stronger was our time with Jesus. We began to treasure this time of pressing into Him. As we seek Him and His perfect will, we began asking Him:

1) Is He stripping us of everything, so we can be more useful for the Kingdom work He has in mind?

2) Is He giving us circumstances to push us back home to the U.S.

3) Or is the Deceivers trying to sift us like wheat, knowing we are a great enemy of hell.

We can endure anything as long as we know it is His will. We do not want to make any decision based on circumstances, so we pray and wait. We have learned that trials and brokenness are the perfect conditions for His greatest work. We know God shines brightest in the dark.

**October 2018:**

In His timing, God has always turned our defeats into victories and this time is no exception. We can see how God is using us wherever we go as if we were walking sanctuaries for His people. Our greatest joy so far is that we have been given a wonderful opportunity to come alongside a feeding center in the slums of Mombasa. We are able to do the equivalent of a VBS for over 500 orphans every Saturday.

Over half of the children come from Muslim homes, so they are not allowed into the church building. But they are looking through the doors and windows and they are listening! We get to do this! Wow! We are overwhelmed that God would let us be a part of something so beautiful. We get to plant seeds of His Word into the hearts of Muslim children and seeds of love into the hearts of the orphans.

We still have our waves of homesickness (especially for our grandson Elliot). I still get butterflies in my stomach when I go on state to ministry. But we take that empty spot that God has left opened for us, and He allows us to pour out His love and goodness onto the treasured ones He puts in our paths.

We are constantly being molded into new creations every day through our trials and sufferings. We are learning to just do what God shows us for today. Our greatest calling is to love Him and His Children, and if we get that right, He works out the rest.

"If all struggles and sufferings were eliminated, the spirit would no more reach maturity than would a child." - Elizabeth Elliot

To learn more about our African missionary work, you can find us on Facebook at <u>Andrus Family Mission</u> and check out our website, <u>www.gosendjoin.us</u>. We would love for you to be involved with our ministry through your support and prayer. Thank you for purchasing and sharing this book. We know your donation will bless the lives of many.

Wayne, Tammy and Haven Andrus

# Writers

**Tammy Andrus** is the 49-year-old mother of four beautiful girls ages 10 to 29 years, the bragging grandmother to one grandson and another grandchild on the way. She completely adores her family along with her husband, Wayne of 22 years. She is so thankful to a husband who balances her procrastinating, dreaming, often forgetful, fly by the seat of her pants attitude. She has no extraordinary gifts except for the gifts of mercy and love. She does not take these gifts lightly because with these small gifts, through Jesus, she can move mountains! With her husband and 10-year-old daughter Haven by her side she is planting seeds of Jesus love into the hearts of the orphan and the most needy. Through ministries like the feeding center, 500 club, baby ministry and bible studies she has seen many lives redeemed. She is a perfect example of how Jesus uses the most ordinary to do the extraordinary. You can find her at her family's African Mission website: http://gosendjoin.us/

**Willow Andrus** attends International House of Prayer University as she prepares for a life of full-time mission work. When she can, she helps her missionary parents in Kenya, Africa, serving the impoverished people of Mombasa.

**Teresa Ann** is the founder and talk show host of <u>LET's Talk with Teresa Ann</u>♡ via both her podcast and <u>YouTube</u> channels. She is also a self-published author of the book, God is Enthralled by Your Beauty, and the blogs <u>Triumphant Victorious Reminders</u> and <u>The Pee Diaries of a Laughing</u> Mom. She LOVES using many adjectives and truly enjoys exploring the scenic route when telling a story! She is known for her loud laughter, yet God's gentle words as she echoes His Word into the hearts of women to simply point them back to the Father GOD. Her heart's desire is that women will begin to see into the mirror of God's Word. Every chance she gets, she loves to come alongside her daughter to minister to everyday people while they help them to discover the treasures of God and convey just how extraordinary God has made them. She enjoys articulating how our lives are to be a sign, wonder and miracle that point others to the Father GOD as HE flips the script in our lives to see no longer from the place of lack but from GOD'S abundant life! You can find Teresa at her website, <u>https://letstalkstudio.com</u>.

**Vicki Beck** is a wife, mother and grandmother, Vicki's greatest joy is spending time with her family. She and her husband, Bill, live in Corpus Christi, Texas, and enjoy the outdoors, gardening, music and exploring the Texas Hill Country on their Harley!

**Maryleigh Bucher** is a wife of 34 years, a mom of five sons ranging in ages from 32 to 17, a Muddy to three grandchildren. She is a Christian woman raising sons to be strong, manly men who love God and show the love of Jesus Christ to others through their words and actions. An encourager, a mother constantly seeking solutions to challenges, a planter of flowers, washer of the blue cotton blanket, and a daughter of the King, made whole in a way she never thought she could be. Maryleigh earned degrees in Journalism and English; homeschooled and taught college students for 20+ years; author of five children's books; blogger at Blue Cotton Memory: The Faith, Love and Politics of Raising Boys to Men. As a mother, her mission statement is to live, showing her boys how to grow old loving the Lord. As a Daughter of the King it's to let others know that they, too, are Daughters of the King and what that means.

**Laura Campise** is a devoted wife and loving mother of three beautiful children. Over the years, she has taught Bible studies, co-chaired a mission committee, and lead home fellowship groups. In her free time, Laura enjoys travelling, immersing herself in new cultures, and meeting new people.

**Kathy Cheek** and her husband live in a Dallas, Texas suburb and have two daughters, one son-in-law and a grandson who also reside in the area.

After more than a decade as a freelance writer in the Christian market including LifeWay, Walk Thru the Bible, David C Cook, and Group Publishing, God has opened the door for Kathy to see her book, First Breath of Morning – Where God Waits For You Every Day - A 90 Day Devotional published in 2018.

First Breath of Morning – Where God Waits For You Every Day – A 90 Day Devotional uniquely formatted in six chapters that portray our walk with God through drawing near, building our relationship, leaning into His love, growing our faith, trusting Him through every circumstance, and exalting Him in worship. First Breath of Morning is an Invitation to the relationship God wants to have with us and it starts in the first breath of each new morning where He is already waiting for you.

You can also read Kathy's devotions on her site *Devotions from the Heart* at www.kathycheek.com

**Felecia Clark** believes that God uses all the experiences of her life to bring her closer to Him and to share what she learns with others. She attempts to follow Paul's example in 1 Thessalonians 2:12 "… encouraging, comforting and urging you to live lives worthy of God, who calls you into his kingdom and glory." Felecia won Honorable Mention for her short story "A Matter of Conscience" in Two Letter Press' 2014 Flash Card Fiction contest. Additionally, her short story "Downward Spiral" earned an Honorable Mention in the Short Story Challenge by NYCMidnight in 2015.

"Are you Ready" is her memoir and debut work which will be available at the end of 2018. Felecia authors the popular Christian blog ALifeSanctified.com and shares her photography with the world at FBDOphotography.com. You can contact her at Felecia@alifesanctified.com.

**Ann Cornelius** is as an Occupational Health Nurse (RN) for 30 years. Her family comes from a long line of preachers, teachers and nurses. Her career was in Houston. She moved to Corpus Christi when her husband retired in 2002.

**Jeannie De La Garza** was passionate about God, her family, and helping others. Born in Topeka, Kansas, she moved to Corpus Christi, Texas, when she was 12 years old. There she met and later married her high school sweetheart, Juan De La Garza. They were married for 36 years and had three beautiful children, nine grandchildren, and three great-grandchildren. Jeannie was active in women's ministries, a contributor to *Granola Bar Devotionals*, and hosted women's Bible studies in her home. One of her greatest joys came from ministering to those in emotional, spiritual, or physical need. Like a beacon in the dark, she radiated God's love, encouragement, and compassion to all of those around her. Although she is no longer with us on this earth, her legacy continues to live on through her family and all those whose lives she touched.

**Angelica Estrada** is hard-working grocery store manager and a full time follower of Jesus. In her free time, Angelica enjoys spending time with her two children and loving husband of 22 years.

**Dr. Cynthia Faulkner** is a Licensed Clinical Social Worker (LCSW) and Professor of Social Work and Program Director for Indiana Wesleyan University's online MSW Program. She and her husband, Sam, live in Texas where they are surrounded by their amazing children, grandchildren, and great-grandchildren. They are also co-authors of Research Methods: A Practice-Based Approach (3rd ed) and Addictions Counseling: A Competency-Based Approach, both published by Oxford University Press. Dr. Faulkner feels that her greatest personal blessings are her children and her greatest professional legacy is her work towards improving the conditions of humankind, "Jesus was the first social worker."

**Cheryl Grundy** has been with Granola Bar Devotionals since the beginning in 2006, God has had her on a fantastic journey! At that time Cheryl was a life group coordinator for what is now Church Unlimited in Corpus Christi. After several missionary trips to Central America to help install water wells and teach health and hygiene and the living water of Christ to villagers in Nicaragua,

Guatemala, and Mexico she was asked to teach the health and hygiene class to prospective missionaries for Living water international In Texas and Washington DC. Moving to Kerrville in 2009, Cheryl's husband, Doyle and her founded Triple R Retreat and Ministries (a 501c3 religious organization) hosting over 4500 souls needing Rest, Relaxation, and Renewal in Christ. Currently they are pastors and directors for that ministry and in addition serve as Chaplains for patients and staff at Kerrville State Hospital, Peterson Regional Hospital, and to employees of client companies for Marketplace Chaplains. Loving the Lord and sharing His Love and Grace is her passion.

**Joan Hall** has appeared in a variety of on-line publications, in the book, Life Lessons from Teachers (available through Amazon), and in The Secret Place devotional. She is also the author of two full-length novels, a novella, and several short stories. She and her husband live in Texas with their three cats. To learn more about Joan, visit her website www.joanhall.net.

**Kerry Johnson** has had a love affair with stories since she was a little girl. She worked in Public Broadcasting while earning her B.S. in English Education from the University of South Florida, then taught middle school remedial reading and drama before spending eight years as a stay-at-home mom and wife. She has been published in Creation Illustrated, Granola Bar Devotionals, and was a regular contributor to Tampa Bay's Overflow Magazine from 2011-2013. In 2008 Kerry began writing her first story, and she dipped her toes in the blogosphere the following year. After nearly a decade of learning the craft of fiction, prayer, and (im)patience, God cracked opened the door she'd eagerly knocked on for years. Her contemporary romance, The Name Game, was a two-time finalist in ACFW's (American Christian Fiction Writers) Genesis Contest (2016 and 2017), and her middle grade manuscript finaled in 2015 then won the Genesis Award in 2017 (YA). In 2016 and 2018, two of Kerry's manuscripts won their categories at the Florida Christian Writers Conference (Middle Grade and Romance). Kerry lives, writes, and sips tea in sunny, stormy Tampa Bay with her patient engineer husband, two active boys, and way too many books. Her prayer is that readers will finish her stories with a smile and a sigh. You can find Kerry at her blog ,https://candidkerry.wordpress.com.

**Jennifer Keller is** currently a Florida resident, living with her loving husband who recently retired from the United States Navy. They are proud parents of three beautiful children, who she gets the pleasure of homeschooling. Jennifer enjoys cooking delicious meals for her family and spending days at the beach. Her motto in life is to skip prepositions and interjections, so they can enjoy the adventures of life. She is currently a full-time student at Liberty University with the goal of obtain a Bachelor's degree in Youth Ministry. Her goal is to build up the youth of today to appreciate their identity in Christ and help them to feel confident in today's society. Her number one passion in life is to serve people to advance the Kingdom of God.

**Christina Ketchum** is an informal gal fueled by faith, love, joy and coffee. Clinical Social Worker trying to help others as much as possible. As a divorced mom of three amazing kiddos, she is living each day in God's grace and love.

**Tiffany Locke** is from Corpus Christi, Texas. She have been married for over 25 years and has two adult daughters and a teenage boy. She calls him her little Russian blessing where they adopted him at six months old from Russia. She is a writer and blogger. She shares her wisdom and offers encouragement and love from a Christian view to pilot wives in the many Takeoff and Landings she experience. You can fly over to visit Tiffany at takeoffandlandings.net.

**Monica Lugo** is a singer, songwriter and worship leader. She has led worship at church almost all of her adult life, singing, playing the guitar and creating a spirit-filled atmosphere. She and her husband, Isai, now reside in Tennessee, writing music and performing around the country. Her first born, Jesse, is now an energetic toddler, and he keeps her busy with his sweet shenanigans.

**Sofia J. Lyons** is a professional singer/songwriter. She resides in Los Angeles California with her husband Jay and their two children Juliana and Felix. Her website is www.sofiaj.com.

**Sara McDaniel** was born and raised in Springhill, Louisiana, and later living in Arkansas, Utah and Texas. Sara recently returned to Louisiana and restored a 1926 historic home. A senior educational consultant by day, Sara blogs, reads and dabbles in real estate investing at night. On her popular blog, SimplySara.com, Sara shares her journey of grace, forgiveness, faith and hope. Sara also blogs at SimplySouthernCottage.com to document the renovation of her historic home. Sara's heartbeat is building community while serving others. She never turns down a good cup of coffee, an opportunity to get outdoors or the ability to help others meet Jesus. You can find Sara at SimplySara.com and SimplySouthernCottage.com.

**Robin McNaueal** has a passion for her family, her dogs, & her country. Hailing from Canada, she recently moved back to her beloved British Columbia from Texas, where she made lifelong friends. Traveling the globe in search of adventure, delving into great fiction, freelance editing, & a budding interest in painting keep her busy when not pursuing her career as an RN. She hopes to add author to that list in the not-too-distant future.

**Tiffany Molina**, educator of 13 years, wife of 15 years to Eliodoro Molina, two beautiful boys, ages 14 and 10. We are a proud military family serving our country for 20 years. We are learning to walk with God, living humbly, happy and healthy.

**Lynn Mosher** has had her socked-feet firmly planted in the Midwest since she drew her first breath. She lives with her hubby (since 1966) in their family nest, emptied now of three chicklets and embracing two giggly grand-chicklets. Although illness has been a part of her life for many years, her deepest passion is sharing her devotionals and modern-day parables to encourage others and glorify the Lord. You can find her online at lynnmosher.com.

**Susie Mozisek** has been married to Creative Arts Pastor, Skip Mozisek, for 26 years. They have three amazing adult children. Susie has been a teacher for 13 years, as well as a Sunday school teacher for over 20 years. Her passion is sharing the love of Jesus to women and young children.

**Liette Ocker** is a wife and mother, driven and passionate. She is an Ironman triathlete and fitness fanatic. After earning a Ph.D. in measurement and assessment of human performance, Liette worked over 15 years as a university professor in statistic and research. She led a major university department and thought she was in her personal and professional sweet spot; God had other plans. During that time, Liette was diagnosed with aggressive breast cancer and everything changed. During treatment God stripped away the noise and showed her He's the sweet spot. Now Liette is attending Harvard Business Analytics, left academics, and has started her own company. She spends every moment possible with her family and friends, and takes time to smell the roses. She is thankful for the God's storm that showed her His light.

**A.J. Pattengill** was born with severe hearing loss not able to hear or speak. A.J. received her first hearing aids at the age 6, and another 12 years of speech therapy. A. J. is an Ordained Minister, started a music ministry "Sounds of Love" in Central America. A.J.'s music ministry reaches out to the hearing and the deaf people in Guatemala. A.J. teaches violin, viola music that communicates love of Jesus Christ.

**Dixie Phillips** is a pastor's wife and Dove Award winning songwriter. She and her husband, Paul, have four married children and fourteen "perfect" grandchildren. They have served the Gospel Lighthouse Church in Floyd, Iowa, for thirty-seven years.

**Lindsey Plumleigh** is a full time stay at home mom in Mansfield, Texas. Nine years ago, Lindsey married her best friend and favorite teammate, Jason Plumleigh. They have two beautiful children, Brody Bear five and Brooke Bee three. Her passion is working with schools and churches to create safe, loving, and inspiring environments for children to learn and grow. On the weekends, you can find Lindsey's family eating breakfast tacos and browsing garage sales.

**Sunny Reed** is married with 3 kids in Austin, TX. She loves reading and coffee and growing the local church. Sunny is a firm believer that Jesus is for everyone and that the local church is the hands and feet of Jesus in every community. Connect with Sunny at reedsunnyc@yahoo.com.

**Kimberly Dawn Rempel** is the author of Garden Meditations and founder of Marketing Mastery for Writers, Kimberly encourages writers and entrepreneurs. Join her free Facebook group, Marketing Mastery for Writers: https://www.facebook.com/KimberlyDawnRempelWriter Editor/

**Tasha Schaded** is married to her best friend, mother of three amazing children, personal trainer, owns and runs multiple businesses, natural figure professional, worship leader, and a lifelong encourager of fitness and faith! You can find her at https://www.facebook.com/lifefitpts/

**DeeDee Sharon** is married to her high school sweetheart and has two fabulous sons. Seven grandchildren call her GiGi and she hosts regular sleepovers. She is passionate about her faith and her family and is best known for that one time she conquered cancer. Sometimes she posts over at deedeesharon.com.

**Susan Chamberlain Shipe**, a writer since the age of eight when she and her neighborhood friend wrote, edited, published, and distributed *The Manor News*. Things have changed since publishing with the five and dime stamp lettering set! The Lord delivered a message of Hope deep within Susan's soul in 2002. Jesus, the Hope-giver met her in her hour of need and her heart overflowed with hope. Susan is the mom of three adult children, grandmother (aka Mimzy) to Hannah and Simon. Today, Susan enjoys blogging, writing short devotions and short stories from her downtown flat in central North Carolina, which she shares with her husband of thirty-plus years, Lowell.

She can be found musing weekly at www.hopehearthome.com. Her life's purpose: That I may walk worthy of the Lord, fully pleasing Him, being fruitful in every good work and increasing in the knowledge of God. Colossians 1:10 (NKJV) Her life vision: I have no greater joy than to hear that my children walk in Truth. 3 John 4

**Erica Skattebo** is a former military kid married to her high school sweetheart who happens to be the best coffee guy in town, and a mom to a son and daughter hand-picked through the blessing of adoption. She is passionate about using God's gift of words to encourage others through her poetry, blog posts, devotionals, and inspirational writings. She's currently working on two other stories from her heart, and prays that each one is God's story, filled with God's words, perfectly pieced together just like her family.

**Tammi Slavin** is a native of South Texas, which she has called "home" her whole life. She has three children and three grandchildren—it is notable to mention they are the best kids & grandkids on the planet (no bias of course!). She is an Occupational Therapist, specializing in hand therapy, and attended UT Medical Branch at Galveston. She has had the honor in assisting many patients over the years with their rehabilitation, and has learned more from her patients than she has "taught." Some of her interests are spending time with family/friends, being ridiculously competitive with family board games, exercising, playing the piano, going on "drive-ventures" with her kids, reading, and learning as much as possible in general. She spends an inordinate amount of time pondering life in general and planning her next prank on her kids in particular. She had the privilege to become involved with the *Granola Bar Devotional* in 2006, in which she was and now continues to be blessed far beyond her small contribution.

**Estella Smith** was raised in the small town of Hendersonville, NC, to a world traveler, by God's Planned Journey. Estella is a military wife married for almost 18 years, and mother to three wonderful children. Homeschooling is her newest adventure and being on God's Wonderful path, always leads her family on new adventures.

**Holly Smith** loves being the wife of Chris (for 27 years!) and mom to Noah (20), Kylie (18), Tabor (15) and Sydney (11). God has gifted Holly with a love of all things creative—from painting and wall-papering to scrapbooking and design work—as well as a love for all people. Recently, she has laid down her web designing cap for her writer's pen, which is her favorite form of art, especially communicating the love and work of Jesus in a way that reaches across all divides. She serves weekly at a local, federal, women's prison, as one of a team of three, teaching a faith-based parenting class. It is her highest joy, seeing these women "get it"—Jesus loves me, yes even me! She carries the stories of people in her heart and she prays for them, even many years later, anticipating the day she will meet them again to hear the great things God has done in their lives. She lives to tell, in every season, God is faithful!

**Alene Snodgrass** is an encourager, writer, traveler, beach lover, but most importantly a Jesus follower. She has published a few books including Dirty Laundry Secrets-a journey to meet the Launderer and Graffiti, which she coauthored with her homeless friend. You can find her on Facebook, Instagram, and at www.positivelyalene.com.

**Stacey Tuley** has been happily and faithfully married for 24 years to her husband Richard, she is the mother of two amazing adult children and two babies she will meet someday in heaven, she has two loyal fur babies as well. She has worked professionally as a BSN, RN who graduated with honors from UTMB-Galveston, Texas. She has been blessed to be an extension of Jesus's arms and feet in both professional (in the areas of newborn nursing, med-surg, hospice, and ob-gyn nursing) and in volunteer ministry settings (as a Celebrate Recovery Women's Step Study Leader for 10 years, Pregnancy Center of the Coastal Bend nurse sonographer, and she started the Beauty for Ashes Ministry in Lake Jackson, Texas in 1999 at Family Life Church that still runs with the same vision, and she has lead and participated in different small group ministry opportunities. She is a Severe Pre-eclampsia with HELLP Syndrome and stroke survivor and thriver. She suffers with rare disease and is a volunteer in the CVID and PI TEXAS online Facebook support group, but she doesn't let it steal her joy, in fact her hardships have molded her to become an unshakable, immovable rock in her faith and an encourager to all she meets who struggle as a by product. She is willing to immediately pray with anyone needing prayer. Her source of strength is found in the Lord, the anchor of her soul.

**Alisa Hope Wagner** loves deep simplicity. She is home most days, but if you do see her out and about, you may actually be face-to-face with her extroverted identical twin sister. More than anything, Alisa adores being a wife to her high school sweetheart, mother to her three awesome children and daughter of the Most-High King. After hours of writing at her computer, Alisa cannot wait to workout in her garage gym. When the day's work is finally done, she listens to smooth jazz and gets creative in the kitchen. Alisa writes across genres, including her four favorite topics—faith, family, fitness and fiction. You can find Alisa's books and devotionals on Amazon and read what the Holy Spirit's been teaching her at her blog, www.alisahopewagner.com.

**Susan Wood** has a unique career traveling throughout the US with her husband, Jonathan, performing raptor presentations and shows. She is author of two books on raptors: *Raptor Basics for Kids Young and Old* and *Raptor Basics - Owls.* Susan also documents the wonderful life lessons that Jesus has taught her over the years, calling them her precious jewels, and she shares these jewels in articles, blogs and person to person.

**Bernadine Zimmerman** is a work in progress whose desire is to live a life that honors God and to tell others of His love for them. She is from a small town on the beautiful island of Grand Bahama but moved to the big city of Dallas, Texas, in 2015 after marrying her husband, Mark. Bernadine is a quietly opinionated bookworm who also loves to write. She can often be found curled up in her favorite chair reading or jotting her thoughts down in one of her many journals. She has written a Bible study for young ladies entitled, *Becoming His Dream Girl*, which can be purchased on Amazon.